T0033508

A GIFT FOR:

....

FROM:

....

DATE:

....

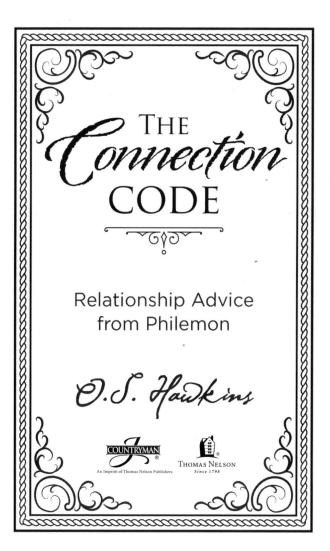

THE
Connection
CODE

Relationship Advice
from Philemon

O. S. Hawkins

COUNTRYMAN
®
An Imprint of Thomas Nelson Publishers

THOMAS NELSON
®
Since 1798

CONTENTS

INTRODUCTION

*S*elf-help books are a dime a dozen in our world today. Search for them in online booksellers or step into a bookstore and you will find them by the hundreds. We have an insatiable thirst to stay ahead of the competition to devour the latest "spin" on self-improvement. However, the more advanced we try to be in modern technique, the more we discover that the best ideas and methodologies have already been tried and tested for centuries. They are simply in need of being repackaged and applied to our more contemporary culture. For example, consider that one of the bestselling management books of the past generation was *The Leadership Secrets of Attila the Hun*. Wess Roberts simply reached back into the past and brought someone to life who had been relegated to ancient history as sort of a barbaric little tyrant. The very principles he used so long ago to motivate and mobilize his motley forces into a nation of Huns with a spirit of conquest are now found to be appropriately accurate and applicable in our world today.

Along the same lines, consider the generational marketing success of the bestseller *The Art of War* by the ancient Chinese warrior Sun Tzu. The strategies and management principles of this warrior-philosopher of 2,500 years ago have found their way into the briefcases and war rooms of practically every business executive in America.

Now, once again, from out of the past, comes an ancient document, a piece of personal correspondence, written by a "people-strategist" to a wealthy entrepreneur almost two thousand years ago. It contains only twenty-five verses in a half dozen or so paragraphs, and yet it is the most articulate case study in the building of positive and productive interpersonal relationships to be found anywhere at any time. Fortunately, this ancient document, known simply as "Philemon," has found its way into the New Testament, thus to be preserved and read for all posterity.

Philemon was a successful business executive in the first-century city of Colosse. This letter involves the relationship between him and two other players. Paul, the letter's author, was writing from a prison cell in Rome where he had been incarcerated for his allegiance to a new and growing phenomenon called Christianity. Onesimus,

the final person in this trio, had been a bond servant of the more influential and wealthy Philemon.

The substance of the letter regards the dynamics of their relationships. Onesimus had stolen from Philemon and split the scene, making his way to Rome and the bright lights of the big city. By the strangest of coincidences, he was arrested by the authorities on an unrelated charge and placed in the same holding cell as Paul. To make matters more "coincidental," Paul happened to be a personal friend of Philemon and had, in fact, won him to faith in Christ on a recent visit to Colosse. In the constant presence of this warm and winsome people person, Onesimus himself soon came to see the error of his ways and also came to a transformational experience through faith in Christ. The proof of this emerged in the fact that upon his release from jail, his intent was to return to Colosse, show Philemon he was remorseful, and seek to make restitution.

With this bit of informational background, we now come to the letter at hand. Paul wrote this letter to Philemon to pave the way for Onesimus's return. It is a blueprint for building positive, productive interpersonal relationships. In this piece of private correspondence, each of the six paragraphs contains a vital element in the building and sustaining of productive relationships.

First, Paul spoke of the importance of affirmation, a pat on the back. Early on in the letter he affirmed Philemon by saying, "Your love has given me great joy and encouragement, because you, brother, have refreshed the hearts of the Lord's people" (Philemon v. 7 NIV). Positive words of honest affirmation have a disarming effect.

He continued with the importance of accommodation, popularly called the "win-win principle," in our interpersonal relationships by reminding Philemon that "formerly he [Onesimus] was useless to you, but now he has become useful both to you and to me" (v. 11 NIV). In our modern vernacular, Paul was approaching him on the basis of a mutually beneficial relationship.

Paul also spoke of the importance of acceptance and forgiveness by calling upon his friend to "receive [Onesimus] as you would me" (v. 17).

No dissertation on interpersonal relationships would be complete without a word about allegiance, and thus Paul proved his commitment to them both by stating to Philemon, "If he has done you any wrong or owes you anything, charge it to me" (v. 18 NIV).

Finally, the apostle addressed the necessity of accountability in our relationships. This is the missing element in so many close connections.

Paul closed the letter, saying, "And one thing more: Prepare a guest room for me, because I hope to be restored to you in answer to your prayers" (v. 22 NIV). In other words, "I am coming by to check up on things and to hold you both accountable in your relationships to each other."

There is much on the market and on the bookstore shelves on building better relationships. Scores of writers each have their own formulas and catchy slogans to motivate and sometimes manipulate people into relationships. Some teach manipulative maneuvers to stimulate others to notice us. There are volumes telling us how to dress and how to win friends to our persuasion. Others even offer suggestions on how to intimidate our way into relationships that can become beneficial to us. Still other books imply we should fake interest in certain hobbies or the interests of others in order to gain influence. When it comes to the bottom line, many of today's modern methods of building productive relationships are superficial and deceptive, resulting in short-term gain at best. The intent of *The Connection Code*, and the content of Philemon's letter, is not just to win friends but to keep them in long-term, mutually beneficial, positive, productive interpersonal relationships.

Life itself is made up of relationships. Each new day

> Life itself is made up of relationships.

brings the need for constructive interpersonal communication. Perhaps this day faces you with the need of making a complaint to a landlord or coping with a problem with someone in your social circle. All of life is about relationships . . . husbands and wives seeking to build better understanding, teachers seeking to translate truth to their students, athletes striving to please the coach. Life is about relationships, and some of us have had great heartache and others of us have caused great heartache because we have never learned how to relate to one another in positive and productive ways. It matters not whether it is in the home, the workplace, or the social arena—we can all profit from learning how to properly relate to one another. Turn the page as, together, we dissect this ancient piece of private, personal correspondence, explore the well-worn secrets to building positive and productive relationships, and unlock . . . the Connection Code.

THE LETTER

A.D. 60

*P*aul, a prisoner of Christ Jesus, and Timothy our brother,

To Philemon our beloved friend and fellow laborer, to the beloved Apphia, Archippus our fellow soldier, and to the church in your house:

Grace to you and peace from God our Father and the Lord Jesus Christ.

I thank my God, making mention of you always in my prayers, hearing of your love and faith which you have toward the Lord Jesus and toward all the saints, that the sharing of your faith may become effective by the acknowledgment of every good thing which is in you in Christ Jesus. For we have great joy and consolation in your love, because the hearts of the saints have been refreshed by you, brother.

Therefore, though I might be very bold in Christ to command you what is fitting, yet for love's sake I rather appeal to you—being such a one as Paul, the aged, and now

also a prisoner of Jesus Christ—I appeal to you for my son Onesimus, whom I have begotten while in my chains, who once was unprofitable to you, but now is profitable to you and to me.

I am sending him back. You therefore receive him, that is, my own heart, whom I wished to keep with me, that on your behalf he might minister to me in my chains for the gospel. But without your consent I wanted to do nothing, that your good deed might not be by compulsion, as it were, but voluntary.

For perhaps he departed for a while for this purpose, that you might receive him forever, no longer as a slave but more than a slave—a beloved brother, especially to me but how much more to you, both in the flesh and in the Lord.

If then you count me as a partner, receive him as you would me. But if he has wronged you or owes anything, put that on my account. I, Paul, am writing with my own hand. I will repay—not to mention to you that you owe me even your own self besides. Yes, brother, let me have joy from you in the Lord; refresh my heart in the Lord.

Having confidence in your obedience, I write to you, knowing that you will do even more than I say. But, meanwhile, also prepare a guest room for me, for I trust that through your prayers I shall be granted to you.

Epaphras, my fellow prisoner in Christ Jesus, greets you, as do Mark, Aristarchus, Demas, Luke, my fellow laborers.

The grace of our Lord Jesus Christ be with your spirit. Amen.

PART 1

LIFE IS ABOUT RELATIONSHIPS

*Paul, a prisoner of Christ Jesus, and Timothy our brother,
to Philemon our beloved friend and fellow laborer, to the
beloved Apphia, Archippus our fellow soldier, and to the
church in your house: Grace to you and peace from God
our Father and the Lord Jesus Christ.*

—PHILEMON 1–3

I have always been an early riser. It matters not whether I go to bed late or early or whether I am rested or worn-out; my internal clock always wakes me up before sunrise. During my pastoral days in Fort Lauderdale, Florida, on the East Coast, I journeyed to San Francisco, on the West Coast, for a speaking engagement. I arrived, had dinner, and went to bed in the hotel to get rest before my assignment the next morning. Like clockwork I was wide awake at 6 a.m. The only problem was I

was now on Pacific time, three hours earlier than my body clock. The little red numerals on the clock radio beside my bed greeted me with the news: 3 a.m.! With zero success, I tried my best to go back to sleep. I quoted every verse I knew and, yes, even began to count sheep jumping over the fence. But all to no avail.

I got up and went to the desk by the window to work on some items I had brought in my briefcase. I reached for the switch to turn on the desk lamp, moved it to the on position . . . and nothing happened. I don't usually give up on things too easily, so I began to do a little detective work. I arrived at the brilliant conclusion that the lamp had only three possible points of connection: the source, the switch, and the socket. I checked the source. The lamp cord was plugged in to the outlet all right, snugly connected to the source. Next, I rechecked the switch. It was turned on. Now the process of deduction was coming to fruition. There was only one more possibility. I checked the socket where the light bulb was screwed into the lamp. Bingo! The bulb must have just been replaced and had not been screwed tightly enough into the socket. I gave it a couple of turns, and there was light!

When we really think about it, life is a lot like that lamp. We have all known people who seem to have a little sparkle or shine about them. And most of us have been connected with others who, by their very presence, light up our lives and the lives of those with whom they come in touch. What is it about these kinds of people? They are connected at the source, the switch, and the socket. There are only three relationships in life. We have relationships with others, whether at home, at the office, in the social arena, or wherever. This is the outward connection, the socket, if you please. Here we make contact and touch the lives of others.

Second, we have a relationship with ourselves. Some call it self-esteem, self-worth, or self-respect. This is the inward connection, the switch that turns on the light. Here we connect with ourselves in order to produce positive relationships with others.

Finally, and this is an awesome thought, we have the capacity to have a personal relationship with God through the Lord Jesus Christ. This is the upward connection, the source where we can plug in to supernatural power.

> We have the capacity to have a personal relationship with God through the Lord Jesus Christ.

What is the bottom line of these three relationships in life: the outward connection, the inward connection, and

the upward connection? We will never properly relate to others until we properly relate to ourselves, and we will never properly relate to ourselves until we find our self-worth in Christ by being connected with Him through faith. In short, in order to shine and light up the lives of others in positive, productive interpersonal relationships, we need to be connected at the source, the switch, and the socket.

We are made to communicate positively with each other in relationships. Back at the very beginning of the created order, with each creative act, God would pause and speak. Do you remember what He said? *That's good.* He said this same thing when He made the sun, the moon, and the stars and put them in their places of orbit in clock-like precision. He said this when He divided the sea and land and made the vegetation and the animal life. *That's good . . . that's good . . . that's good.* But then He made man, and God said something else: "Not good"! What? "It is not good that man should be alone" (Genesis 2:18). We are made to connect with each other in the power of productive interpersonal relationships. By our very nature, we are made to connect with each other. Much of our success in life is not determined by how much we know or how high we have managed to climb in material circles, but in

our ability to build positive, productive relationships with others in the home, in the marketplace, and in the social arena.

Two thousand years ago the apostle Paul laid hold of this threefold principle of relationships and masterfully used it in the initial paragraph in his letter of greeting to his friend Philemon. In the ensuing chapters we will discover how Paul viewed himself as connected at the source, plugged in to an unlimited power supply, fueled by the Holy Spirit. He saw himself as connected at the switch. He was switched on and exuded self-worth, self-respect, and self-confidence by finding his own identity in the person of Jesus Christ. And the result of his being plugged in and switched on was that when he touched the lives of others, he not only brightened their road but had a unique way of lightening their load at the same time.

> Paul viewed himself as connected at the source, plugged in to an unlimited power supply, fueled by the Holy Spirit.

The problem with so many relationships is a breakdown at one of these points of connection. Some have a difficult time relating to others because of the fact that their own self-image is damaged. Thus, their tendency is to be so fearful of rejection that contact is never made with others,

and the light that could mean so much to others never gets switched on. Many relationships are unhealthy because we can project what we feel about ourselves onto other people in our world. Still others seem to move from one relationship to another, never able to move beyond just short-term connections.

Let's rewind the tape a moment. Allow me to say what I have already said and what I intend to repeat throughout the following pages. We have only three relationships in life: an outward expression, an inward expression, and an upward expression. And the truth is, we will never properly relate to others until we properly relate to ourselves. This will never happen until we come into a relationship with God through Jesus Christ, realize how indescribably valuable we are to Him, and begin to find our self-worth in Him—not in ourselves. This is the thrust of Paul's ancient yet applicable letter to Philemon. Let's continue the journey to unlocking the Connection Code.

1 THE ETERNAL CONNECTION

*I*n Paul's opening paragraph of salutation to his friend Philemon, he said, "Grace to you and peace from God our Father" (Philemon v. 3). He revealed much of his own relationship with his source in this initial greeting. As Paul penned these words, he was writing in Greek, which was the universal written language of his day. In order to signal his own relationship with God, he used the Greek word *patros*, which we translate as "Father." He saw himself in a father-and-son relationship with the source of his life.

This same word is used to describe the father in the old and often-repeated story of the Prodigal Son in Luke's gospel. You can find the whole tale in Luke 15:11–32. It is the heartwarming story of the boy who took his inheritance and left home for the bright lights of the big city. It did not take him long to lose it all, along with his dignity and self-respect. What had promised to be a good time brought nothing but rip-offs, back alleys, and unemployment lines. But the story has a happy ending. He decided to get up and go home. What would his father say? Or worse, what would his father do? The same dad who earlier had released the inheritance and let him go now said, *I receive you, and what is more, I reward you.*

The boy's father did not have to let him go in the first place. He could have refused to give him the inheritance money. But there are times when parents know what is ultimately best and let their children go. He released him, but he never gave up on him. When the boy returned with a repentant heart, the father welcomed him back with open arms and even rewarded him for finally doing what was right. All of that is wrapped up in Paul's greeting to Philemon when he used the word "Father."

Father . . . that is a difficult word for some of us to get around. In fact, for many people, that is the very word that is at the root of many unresolved problems in relationships with others. It is an all-too-common reality that some of us have a difficult time relating to others due to our own feelings of inadequate self-confidence and self-worth that are a direct result of unpleasant relationships with our earthly fathers. But Paul was not speaking of an earthly father here. He was visualizing himself in a relationship with his heavenly Father, like that of a loving and supportive

father-and-son relationship as depicted in Jesus' story of the Prodigal Son.

This is a good time to pause a moment to ask a rather personal question: How do you view yourself as being connected to God the Father, your eternal source of power? Positive and productive relationships begin when we see Him as our Father. He releases us. We are not puppets but people. And though He provides us with our own free will, He never gives up on us. The very moment when we are ready to connect, or reconnect, with Him, He receives us with open arms and gives us a brand-new beginning. He will become a source of strength and power to any and all of us who come to Him—especially those of us who may not have had positive relationships with our earthly fathers. This eternal connection, touching our source of being, begins when we, like Paul, see Him as our Father and view ourselves as His own sons and daughters.

> How do you view yourself as being connected to God the Father, your eternal source of power?

Paul continued his greeting in his letter to Philemon, writing, "Grace to you and peace from God our Father and the Lord Jesus Christ" (v. 3). With these words, he introduced an added dimension in this eternal connection. He

now gave this source the name Lord, or *kurios* in the written language of the New Testament. He not only viewed his source of daily power as the paternal one, but also as the prominent one—that is, his Lord. Thus, he demonstrated that he viewed himself not only as a son but also as a servant. Remember, Paul was writing this letter to Philemon expressly in regard to his relationship with one of his servants, Onesimus. With these words, Paul was subtly reminding Philemon that each of us is a child and a servant in our relationships with God. This awareness helps bring our own inward relationship with ourselves and our outward relationships with others into clearer perspective.

Having described his relationship with God as the paternal one (Father) and the prominent one (Lord), Paul went a step further by referring to Him as the Promised One, *Christos*, Christ. For Paul, a learned and aristocratic Jew, he found his source of strength in the long-awaited and promised Messiah, to whom the world had been looking and for whom the world had been waiting for centuries.

Throughout his life in the synagogue and as a member of the Jewish Sanhedrin, Paul had celebrated that high and holy Day of Atonement, Yom Kippur. In Hebrew, *Yom Kippur* means "the day of covering." It was on this holy day that the sins of the previous year were "covered" by the blood of animal sacrifice. Today, our Jewish friends have abandoned their animal sacrifices and see their covering through *mitzvot* (good works). Paul, by referring to the Lord as *Christos*, identified Him as that Promised One who came to become a covering for all our sin and shame; through faith in Him, our faults and failures can bring purpose and peace to our lives.

Paul, in dealing with the source of all relationships, was not speaking about some unknown, unnamed "force" or positive mental attitude, but the person of Jesus Christ Himself. This can best be illustrated by remembering the hotel on the West Coast I mentioned previously. When it came time to check out of the hotel, I did not pull out a wad of cash to pay for my room. I used a credit card. That credit card had no real intrinsic value in and of itself. It was just a piece of plastic. But the hotel clerk accepted my card as if it was cash. Why did she do that? It was a forerunner of the true payment that would come later. The actual payment came a few days later when I paid my credit card bill, and the company forwarded the money on to the hotel. Until then, the credit card simply covered the purchase.

As such, the old covenant between God and man with its sacrificial system "covered" the faults and failures and the sins of those who believed in the Promised One who

21

was coming. And He came! He made the final payment for our covering with the sacrifice of His own life and the shedding of His own blood on a Roman cross of execution outside the city walls of Jerusalem. Consequently, through Christ, our own relationship with the Father has been purchased and secured. It is no wonder our Jewish friends have abandoned their sacrificial systems for the last two thousand years. There is no need for the credit card. The bill has been paid—and paid in full!

> Through Christ, our own relationship with the Father has been purchased and secured.

Paul spoke with authority to Philemon, and to us, regarding interpersonal relationships because he was well-connected. After his conversion, he related well and winsomely to others because he possessed a positive self-image found through his own relationship with Jesus Christ. He found his source of strength in the paternal One (Father) and saw himself as a member of God's forever family. He found his source in the prominent One (Lord) and thus viewed himself as one who was under a higher authority. And he found himself in relationship with the Promised One (Christ), and this set him free to find his own identity in what he described as "Christ in you, the hope of glory"

(Colossians 1:27). This eternal connection brought to Paul indescribable value as an individual and a high sense of self-worth. If we are not properly plugged into our source, the light will never shine through us and into the lives of others.

2 THE INTERNAL CONNECTION

*P*aul recognized the importance of possessing a positive self-image in his relationships with those around him. What is self-image? We are not referring to such things as self-centeredness, self-exaltation, or selfishness. Self-image has to do with such attributes as self-awareness, self-acceptance, self-appreciation, self-worth, self-love, and self-respect. It is the way we image or view ourselves. This is at the very core of many of society's modern ills. Every day we read about problems brought on by drug addiction, violence, prostitution, and many other avenues of social disorder. These are often just the fruits of a much deeper root of low self-esteem, self-respect, and self-worth. A large segment of society has been raised in environments where they never knew affirmation, and it should be no surprise that their lack of self-worth and the low view they have of themselves internally can have disastrous results. It is nearly impossible to relate in positive ways with others externally when we have such little self-esteem internally.

Paul referred to himself in the opening verse of Philemon as a "prisoner of Christ Jesus." In so doing, he was revealing much about his own self-connection. Being a prisoner himself of Nero and the Roman Empire at the time of his writing, he chose an interesting word to describe himself as Christ's prisoner: the Greek word *desmios*. It is of interest to note that in writing to Philemon, he did not say he was a prisoner of Rome. Yet the Romans were the ones who incarcerated him. They were the ones who locked him up. They were the ones who were watching over him. But they were a small part of the larger drama. Paul saw himself primarily as a prisoner of the Lord. He was not there by accident. He had placed his life in God's control and care, and though everyone else considered him a prisoner of Rome, he knew better. He was not a prisoner *for* Christ Jesus; he was a prisoner *of* Christ Jesus. And there is a difference.

Positive and productive interpersonal relationships develop from the inside out. They not only have an external connection, but they also have an internal connection. Like the lamp that gives light, they are not only plugged in at the external source, but they are also turned on at the internal switch. This process of developing relationships from the inside out is a process that we call "being comes

25

before doing," for what we do and how we act in relationship with others is determined by who we are and *whose* we are. For example, if you want to have a more fulfilling marriage, then *be* a more considerate spouse yourself. If you want a teenager in the home to be more cooperative, then *be* a more consistent, loving, and understanding parent. If you want a mom or dad to treat you more fairly, then *be* the kind of son or daughter you ought to be; dust off those old words about honoring and obeying your parents. If you want to have more opportunity for advancement in the workplace, then *be* the most efficient, hardworking, and cooperative employee in the office. In short, if you want to have a good friend, start by *being* a good friend. Paul realized that in order to have a friend like Philemon, he needed to first *be* a friend to him.

> Paul realized that in order to have a friend like Philemon, he needed to first *be* a friend to him.

When we speak of being in touch with ourselves or being connected with ourselves, we are not referring to some New Age concept of self-improvement or self-awareness. Quite the contrary. Jesus had said it like this: "Whoever finds their life will lose it, and whoever loses their life for my sake will find it" (Matthew 10:39 NIV). A powerful and positive self-image does not come from

a pseudo, pumped-up mental attitude. It results from being connected with the Lord in such an intimate way that we become aware of how indescribably valuable we are to Him. Now, what does all this have to do with Paul referring to himself as a "prisoner of Christ Jesus" (v. 1)? There is a sense in which all of us should view ourselves as "prisoners" of our Creator. When we are held captive by His love, it has a liberating effect on our self-image and worth. And aren't we all prisoners of someone or something? Some are held in the prison of their own passions. Others are prisoners of their own popularity. Still others are confined to the prison of pride. Still others are prisoners of another person. The way to a positive sense of true self-worth is to become, in the words of Paul, a "prisoner of Christ Jesus."

This idea, put forth by Christ, of losing ourselves in the Lord Jesus in order to really find our true selves is in diametric opposition to most worldviews today. This is why so many live such confusing and complicated lives. Many have bought into the superficial and deceptive message of our day in a quest to "find themselves." There is only one way to find our true self, and many miss it because of its paradoxical truth: "Whoever finds their life will lose it, and whoever loses their life for my sake will find it." All

of this is in that little Greek word Paul chose to describe himself as a "prisoner of Christ Jesus."

Paul was the single most successful people strategist of his day, and it was because he had a sense of positive self-worth that emanated from being a prisoner of the Lord. He had "lost" his life of popularity and prestige. But he had found so much more that brought not only a purpose to life but also a spirit of conquest. How? He was connected to God, the eternal source. He was plugged into His power and switched on so that this supernatural winsomeness and warmth flowed into him and out of him into the lives of all those with whom he came into contact.

Everything finds its strength from its source. If we are only trying to connect with our self, if the self is the source for us, then we have nothing more than a shallow self-awareness that must constantly be pumping itself up like an old-fashioned surface water pump well behind some dilapidated farmhouse. Some go from one self-help guru to the next, one leadership book to the next, one video series to the next, one seminar to the next, just like a water pump. Pump. Pump. Pump. Pump. But when you get connected to the source with an eternal connection to Jesus Christ and find your self-worth in Him, it becomes like an artesian well. You never have to pump an artesian

well. You just turn on the spigot and it flows because it has been dug deep into the ground and has tapped into an underground river as its source.

> When you get connected to the source with an eternal connection to Jesus Christ and find your self-worth in Him, it becomes like an artesian well.

This is what Paul was saying to Philemon, and to us, as he talked about the importance of this internal connection. The truth is, we are all prisoners of something, and how much better is it to be a prisoner of the source of all living things? This is where we find self-image, self-esteem, self-worth, and self-respect—not in an emotional, pumped-up mental attitude, but in the spiritual realm. In many of Paul's other letters, he said such things as "I can do all things through Christ who strengthens me" (Philippians 4:13). In his letter to the church at Rome, he reminded them that "we are more than conquerors through Him who loved us" (Romans 8:37). How could he make such statements? He had lost his life in the love of his power source and found in Him his inner strength and ability to believe God could make the impossible possible.

The more Paul was connected to his self, the more he saw himself as he really was. This progression played out vividly in his letters in the New Testament. His first

recorded letter was to the people in the region of Galatia and was written in or around AD 49. Here he referred to himself as "an apostle" (Galatians 1:1). Can you imagine him as he sat at his desk and penned these words with perhaps a bit of a puffed-up chest?

Five or six years later he wrote to the church in Corinth and greeted them by saying he was the "least of the apostles" (1 Corinthians 15:9). Later, in AD 60, he wrote the letter we call Ephesians and then referred to himself as "less than the least of all the saints" (Ephesians 3:8). A year or so later he wrote to his friend Philemon and called himself a "prisoner of Christ Jesus."

And a few years later he wrote a moving letter to his young understudy, Timothy, referring to himself as the chief of sinners (1 Timothy 1:15). Most of the world would not recognize this as being a positive self-image. But most of the world seldom looks beyond the surface and the superficial. The more this man lost his life in the love of the source of his strength, the more he found it. And the more he truly found it, the more it took root and bore fruit in his relationships with other people.

> The more this man lost his life in the love of the source of his strength, the more he found it.

So much of our low self-esteem

comes from the influences of those around us. In some cases, this involves parents. In other cases, peers. But what is most important in recovering damaged emotions and feelings of self-worth is not what others think of us but in what God, the ultimate source of all, thinks of us. He loves you just as you are! When you place your trust in Christ, He sees you as His own child. Jesus did not leave His throne in glory to come down and take on human flesh to die on a Roman cross for someone of no worth or little value. You are indescribably valuable to Him. And when you awaken to this reality, you will begin to find your own self-worth where Paul did: "Christ . . . in me" (Galatians 2:20)!

3 THE EXTERNAL CONNECTION

*W*e are social beings who, by our very nature, are made to interact and relate with one another. Like the aforementioned hotel lamp we, too, emit expression when we are connected to our true source of power. When we are in proper relationship with God, we find our self-worth in Him and are then able to spread light to others with whom we come into contact. It is not enough to be plugged in and switched on if we are not connecting with others and letting our light shine. We need each other. God made us that way. We are meant to relate to one another in mutually beneficial ways. Because Paul was properly related to God and to himself, his salutation in his letter to Philemon revealed that he was related to others in four unique and distinctive ways. He began, "Paul, a prisoner of Christ Jesus, and Timothy our brother, to Philemon our beloved friend and fellow laborer, to the beloved Apphia, Achippus our fellow soldier, and to the church in your house" (Philemon vv. 1–2). He saw himself in the external connection of interpersonal relationships as a family member, a friend, a fellow laborer, and a fellow soldier.

First, we need to see each other as family. Paul did. And this was one of the secrets to his success. He built a family consciousness and cohesiveness with those in his inner circle. He spoke of Timothy as his "brother" and in many translations referred to Apphia, most probably Philemon's wife, as his "sister." Paul thought of these individuals not merely as friends but as close members of his family of faith. His constant use of the plural pronoun *our* was no accident. He said, "our brother . . . our beloved friend . . . our fellow laborer . . . our sister . . . our fellow soldier." It is of vital importance in the building of positive relationships that we create a spirit of camaraderie and community. True friendships among believers become family affairs. There is a sense in which we are more closely related to each other through the blood of Christ than to our own blood relatives who do not know Him.

> It is of vital importance in the building of positive relationships that we create a spirit of camaraderie and community.

Second, in this external connection, Paul also saw himself as a friend as well as a member of the family. With much affection he addressed Philemon as his "beloved

friend" (v. 1). Someone has suggested that a genuine friendship is like a beautiful flower—our relationship with others is the fruit, our relationship with ourselves is the shoot, and our relationship with God is the root. This is simply a way of repeating the premise of this paragraph in Philemon—we will never positively and productively relate to others until we develop a proper self-image, and we will never have a confident self-image without properly relating to the Lord Jesus Christ.

Third, Paul continued by seeing himself not only as a member of the family and a friend but as a fellow worker. He used an interesting word, *synergos*, to translate the phrase "fellow laborer." It is a compound word literally meaning to "work with." We derive our English word *synergy* or *synergism* from this ancient Greek word. Synergism describes the combined action of two different agents producing a greater effect than the sum of their individual actions. In plainer terms, it simply means the whole is greater than the sum of the parts.

Take into account two pencils as illustrative of this word. If you hold one in your hands, it is relatively easy to break it in two. However, if you put them together, it becomes exponentially more difficult to break them. With synergism one plus one does not equal two; it equals three or more. In using this word to describe his external connection with Philemon, Paul was showing us how much we need each other and how valuable and strong we become when we are together.

This dynamic is referred to in the Bible when it said that one can chase a thousand, but two can chase ten thousand (Deuteronomy 32:30). This is synergism in action. Jesus once said, "If two of you agree on earth concerning anything that they ask, it will be done for them by My Father in heaven" (Matthew 18:19). The wisest man who ever lived, King Solomon, said it like this: "Two are better than one. . . . For if they fall, one will lift up his companion. . . . if two lie down together, they will keep warm. . . . Though one may be overpowered by another, two can withstand him. And a threefold cord is not quickly broken" (Ecclesiastes 4:9–12).

Paul was a people person and realized the power in working together with others toward a common goal. Effective interpersonal relationships are not the result of competition but of cooperation. "Fellow laborers" share each other's dreams, work together in unity toward the same goal, and share in each other's

> Effective interpersonal relationships are not the result of competition but of cooperation.

victories as if they were their own. All this is behind his referring to Philemon as his "fellow laborer," his *synergos.*

There is a dynamic synergistic power whenever we find two people working together like this. We see it when a mother and a father connect with each other in the parenting process. This is vital for raising positive kids in a negative world. If parents are not together in the discipline of their children, significant damage can be done in the upbringing of the child. However, when they connect and stand together, when one parent always speaks and acts in unison with the other, the child soon gets the lesson, and positive results take place.

Synergism is what takes place when a teacher and a student connect on an assignment. They become "fellow laborers." It happens on the football team when the quarterback and the receiver connect on designed plays and pass patterns. It takes place in the office when brainstorming together creates a culture where new plans and ideas begin to take shape. The epitome of synergy is seen when a bride and a groom leave the wedding altar to become one in Christ. Paul's idea of being a "fellow laborer" with Philemon is an indispensable principle in managing and maintaining positive and productive relationships with others, whether they be found in the home, at the office,

or in the social arena. This external connection involves seeing each other as family, as friends, and as fellow laborers—together.

Last, Paul added one more element to this external connection. He referred to Archippus as a "fellow soldier" (v. 2). This is a very expressive term in Greek that carries with it the idea of being a fellow combatant, a comrade in arms, one who faces the same dangers and fights in the same foxhole as another in the same conflict. As believers, we are all members of the same regiment. Some of us do not see ourselves in the same struggles, looking toward the same victories as others. There seem to be a lot of one-man armies in the marketplace today. Too often in our world, when someone gets wounded in the battle, it is his so-called friends who finish him off with criticism, gossip, or judgment. People in longtime relationships are not only family and friends but "fellow soldiers" in the daily fight.

Life, from beginning to end, is all about relationships. Life is about our relationship with God. It is about our relationship with ourselves. And it is also about our relationships with others. Think of what Christ did in order to connect with us in a vital relationship. He laid aside His glory in heaven. He humbled Himself and came down here where we are. He clothed Himself in a garment

> Life is about our relationship with God. It is about our relationship with ourselves. And it is also about our relationships with others.

of human flesh and for thirty-three years walked among us. He talked with us. He ate with us. He traveled with us. Yet He was never contaminated by our sin. And why did He come? To bring us into a relationship with the Father. This is why earlier Paul had said to the Corinthians that God "has reconciled us to Himself through Jesus Christ, and has given us the ministry of reconciliation" (2 Corinthians 5:18). Getting right with God, being reconciled to Him, is the initial step in building positive and productive relationships with others.

As is so often the case, some of life's greatest lessons show up in relatively small ways and in inconvenient "interruptions" in the simple traffic patterns of our day. In retrospect, I am thankful that lamp in that West Coast hotel room did not come on at three o'clock that morning. If it had, I might have missed a magnificent lesson that has enabled me to relate better to my wife, my children, those in my workplace, and all those with whom I come in contact. We are made to shine with the light of Christ. But until we are plugged in to Him and turn on the switch,

allowing His power to flow through us, we will not light up the lives of those around us.

Positive relationships begin with our relationship with Christ. Turn on the switch, and allow God's love to shine through you to brighten the roads of others.

PART 2

A PAT ON THE BACK

Your love has given me great joy and encouragement, because you, brother, have refreshed the hearts of the Lord's people.

—PHILEMON 7 NIV

*I*t was the 1960s. What a time to be in high school. In fact, I have always felt a tinge of sorrow for those who were not teenagers during the golden oldies days of the sixties. Those were the days of pep rallies and pom-poms, glasspack mufflers and drag races, Bass Weejuns and Levi's, button-down collars and madras windbreakers, hayrides and sock hops, the Beatles, and . . . high school English! When it came time to do my English homework in those days, I would much rather have been where the British pop singer Petula Clark sang about: downtown, where all the lights are bright.

My English teacher's name was Miss Ava White. The emphasis should be placed on the "Miss," not "Mrs.," not "Ms.," but "Miss" Ava White. In those ancient days of yesteryear, she would have been referred to as a "spinster." Never married, she had devoted her entire life to teaching high school students the finer points of the English language and literature. Miss White had developed quite a reputation in my hometown for being a strict, no-nonsense disciplinarian, earning the title of the toughest teacher in the school.

The first half of the semester, I never applied myself. Being overly consumed in all the extracurricular activities afforded me, I seldom studied, had a very active social life, and in my immaturity, sought to simply get by. I remember well the day Miss White announced that she wanted to see me at her desk after class was dismissed. There was no doubt in my mind that I had been caught doing something—or not doing something, like homework. I assumed she was going to give me a piece of her mind for my poor conduct and grades and, most likely, hand me a pink slip with instructions to present myself at the principal's office. I knew what that would mean. I had visited there before on similar occasions. In those days before corporal punishment was banned from

public schools, I had felt the effects of the principal's paddle on my posterior.

As Miss White had demanded, I approached her elevated desk after all my classmates had exited the room. She looked me square in the eyes and said, "Son, you have character. You have a bright mind and are capable of doing far better work in this class than you are doing. I believe in you and have every confidence that you could be an A student if you would just apply yourself." Wow! I could hardly believe my ears. Miss Ava White believed in me! And that simple pat on the back did more for me than I could ever put into words. She agreed to meet with me for a time a few days after school to tutor me. She taught me how to think analytically. She taught me how to outline. In no time, my grades soared from Cs to As. To this very day, decades later, every time I outline a new book or organize a new chapter, I am indebted to Miss Ava White. She believed in me, and she let me know it. She changed the way I thought about myself with one simple pat on the back.

> In building positive and productive interpersonal relationships, affirmation—a pat on the back—is an essential element.

In building positive and productive interpersonal

relationships, affirmation—a pat on the back—is an essential element. Paul's letter to Philemon is a case study in the building of mutually beneficial relationships. In the first paragraph of his letter, following the salutation, he began with a strong word of affirmation of Philemon that opened wide the door for the request he was going to make later in a following paragraph. Try to put yourself in Philemon's place as he began to read the letter and was confronted with these words: "Your love has given me great joy and encouragement, because you, brother, have refreshed the hearts of the Lord's people" (Philemon v. 7 NIV). I imagine that he must have sat up a bit straighter, his chest must have stuck out a bit more, a smile must have appeared on his face, and he was eager to read more. A simple pat on the back can enable a person to change the way they think about themselves and others. It is a eureka moment in unlocking the Connection Code.

4   A WORD OF APPRECIATION

*T*he first step is the most important step in any journey. A lot of relational failures have resulted from getting started on the wrong foot. Some relationships that seemed filled with potential crumbled at the outset through an awkward date or an ill-prepared interview. A pat on the back with an honest note of appreciation has a disarming effect and can play a major role at the beginning of a positive connection. It has a way of setting people at ease and causing them to feel good about themselves. If we take the time to think about it, most of us can attest to times in our lives when some "Ava White" spurred us on to greater heights by giving us a genuine pat on the back.

The lack of positive results in more than one negotiation has occurred at the very point where a lack of mutual affirmation and appreciation by the parties involved has become apparent. This is true not only in the domestic world and the workplace but in the geopolitical realm. Take, for example, the decades-long struggle of the

Israeli-Palestinian issue. If there are seemingly unsolvable conflicts, this one appears to be at the top of the list. This is one situation that has been virtually void of any element of appreciation or affirmation from either side to the other, resulting in year after year of stagnation and standoff. I have often wondered what a difference it might make if the Palestinians acknowledged the horror of the Jewish Holocaust, in which six million Jews were annihilated. And what if the Jews acknowledged the horrors of the massacres at such Palestinian villages as Deir Yassin and Sabra and Shatila? What might happen if, instead of expressing their desire to drive Israel into the sea, the Palestinians recognized Israel's right to exist within defined and secure borders? The other side of the coin would entail Israel's acknowledgment of the Palestinian desire for self-autonomy and self-government in some secure fashion. Could more productive outcomes exist with some genuine words of appreciation from both sides? Perhaps this hope is overly simplistic, but the fact remains that a pat on the back has a disarming effect and can indeed become the launchpad for more productive relationships. There is little hope for successful solutions to any relationship that is void of the element of appreciation.

Realizing the importance of this valuable element,

Paul began his letter to Philemon by reaching across the miles to give him a symbolic pat on the back. Before he ever approached the real message of the letter—to receive Onesimus back—Paul disarmed Philemon by expressing his appreciation of him and saying what an encouragement he has been to him personally. The lack of expressed appreciation in many modern relationships is epidemic. In fact, in our "me" culture, it is an almost extinct commodity. Be honest: When was the last time you intentionally gave someone a genuine pat on the back, a word of positive appreciation and encouragement? When was the last time you sent an email or made a call to someone just to express your affirmation and appreciation of them? A significant contributor to the cultural decay we see in our world today is found in the fact that too many young people were raised without ever hearing a single word of affirmation or appreciation for who they are or what they have done.

We all need a pat on the back from time to time—and even when we do not deserve it. This is truer in the home than anywhere else. When we were raising our daughters, my wife reminded me on more occasions than

> We all need a pat on the back from time to time—and even when we do not deserve it.

I can count that our kids needed our love and appreciation the most when they deserved it the least.

This piece of private correspondence from Paul to Philemon revealed many principles that can be applied to our relationships today. He began by showing that a pat on the back will always involve the element of appreciation: "I thank my God, making mention of you always in my prayers" (Philemon v. 4). Paul was not hesitant nor one bit ashamed to let his friend know he was appreciated. The tense of the verb indicates this was not some arrow shot at random but a sincere word on Paul's behalf. Repeatedly, he expressed his thanks for his friend. The very act of thanksgiving has a liberating effect to it. Someone we know needs to hear this word from us. Perhaps a wife or a husband, a child, or a coworker. Paul wanted Philemon to know that he was appreciated. Verbalizing our appreciation of others is one of the missing elements in relationships today, and its absence is close to the root of many misunderstandings and strained relationships.

Before turning the page to the next chapter, allow God to bring someone to your mind right now to whom you could send a word of appreciation. It just might make their day. And I guarantee you they will not forget you did it.

5   A WORD OF AUTHENTICATION

*B*efore someone gets the erroneous idea that giving a pat on the back to someone is simply some cleverly devised, manipulative maneuver in an attempt to influence another person, Paul made it clear that to be effective, appreciation must be authentic, not artificial. He continued not by simply telling Philemon that he was thankful for him, but by expressing why he was thankful. He said, "Because I hear of your faith in the Lord Jesus and your love for all the saints" (Philemon v. 5 NET).

Honesty is essential in long-term positive and productive relationships. Many secular volumes dealing with relationships that flood the market today are built upon manipulative maneuvers and are often less than honest in their approach to seek to gain leverage over the other party in the relationship. However, most people are wise to this approach. Make sure in building relationships that when you give someone a pat on the back, it is authentic and meaningful, not artificial and manipulative.

Manipulation and false affirmation simply to gain advantage had no place in Paul's approach to building positive relationships. Learn from him. He found a character trait in the life of Philemon to which he could authentically give him a word of appreciation and affirmation. He affirmed both his loyalty and his love. He wrote that he thanked God for Philemon's loyalty and for his personal faith in his Lord. Paul spoke of Philemon's "faith in the Lord Jesus" (v. 5 NET). He also affirmed his love, his positive behavior, by saying he was also thankful for his "love for all the saints" (v. 5 NET).

In the art of building relationships, order is important. Genuine faith in our Lord precedes true love for our friends. Behavior does not come before belief. What we genuinely believe will determine how we generally behave. This sentence in Paul's introductory paragraph of his letter to Philemon was written in the present tense, which indicates that faith and love were not simply manifested in Philemon's past but were ongoing traits of his life.

As I mentioned, once Paul had affirmed his friend's loyalty to the faith, he then affirmed his love for others by writing, "I hear of your . . . love for all the saints" (v. 5

NET). When our faith is authentic, it always manifests itself in love, which becomes the glue that holds together all lasting relationships. Belief determines behavior, for what we do is a response to who we are. When believers display true love for another, it is because of their discovery of how

> When believers display true love for another, it is because of their discovery of how much God loves them.

much God loves them. Philemon's love for all the saints was an authentication of his faith in the Lord Jesus Christ.

It is noteworthy that Paul wrote about Philemon's love for "all" the saints. Philemon built productive relationships because he did not play favorites. He reached out with affirmation not just to those who were popular or prosperous but also to those who were powerless and poor. Do you see what Paul, this master people strategist, was doing? He was finding authentic reasons to give Philemon a genuine pat on the back. It was all legitimate. As Paul wrote, he was thinking ahead a few paragraphs in his epistle. In a few sentences to come, he would bring up the situation with Onesimus. By affirming that Philemon loves "all" the saints, he's including Onesimus, his runaway servant. Incidentally, Onesimus is already on his journey home in repentance and remorse to make restitution. What choice

will Philemon have but to receive him and restore the broken relationship? Nearer to the end of his letter, Paul would say, "If then you count me as a partner, receive him [Onesimus] as you would me" (Philemon v. 17). When Philemon read these words, no doubt Paul's words of authentic affirmation, "love for all the saints," rang in his mind.

A good percentage of Americans indicate they still believe in some type of relationship with God and believe Him to be the source of all being. But the two acid tests of authentic discipleship are found in Paul's words here—a personal belief followed by a positive behavior. Loyalty to Christ and love for others. These are two wings on the same airplane, two sides of the same coin. Like ham and eggs, and steak and potatoes, they appear together. In our increasingly secular age, we are constantly being told it does not matter what we believe as long as we love others and tolerate their aberrant lifestyles. But what we truly believe has its own way of determining how we behave. The apostle John framed it like this: "We know that we have passed from death to life, because we love the brethren. . . . If someone

> Loyalty to Christ and love for others. These are two wings on the same airplane, two sides of the same coin.

says, 'I love God,' and hates his brother, he is a liar" (1 John 3:14; 4:20). Paul's own leader, Jesus of Nazareth, when asked which was the greatest of all the commandments, said that it was loving others out of a genuine love for God (Matthew 22:36–40).

Try to place yourself in Philemon's place as he read this initial paragraph in this intensely personal piece of private correspondence from his mentor in the faith. Paul was reaching out across the miles in this handwritten letter to give Philemon a pat on the back. Word had gotten out. He had heard about all these positive character traits that people had seen in Philemon. I wonder: Has anyone in your sphere of influence heard about your faith in the Lord Jesus or your love for all the saints? Is the word out on you—and me—as it was on Philemon?

A pat on the back is the starting place for building relationships. But it must be authentic in order to be effective. In winning friends and positively influencing others, it is not enough to let them know they *are* appreciated; they must also know *why* they are appreciated. This is not about manipulation. It is all about authentication, honesty in our affirmation of others.

6   A WORD OF ASPIRATION

A genuine pat on the back involves not only the elements of appreciation and authentication, but it also possesses the element of aspiration. Words of affirmation and validation cause us to aspire to loftier goals. Paul continued his letter by stating his desire "that the sharing of your faith may become effective by the acknowledgment of every good thing which is in you in Christ Jesus" (Philemon v. 6). Paul, a master of developing relationships, was now challenging Philemon to be active, not reactive. A pat on the back serves to challenge us to move to greater heights in Christian living. Personal words of affirmation that come our way tend to inspire us to rise higher than we might otherwise. Knowing that someone believes in us has an amazing motivational dimension to it.

Paul wrote, "I pray that your partnership with us in the faith may be effective in deepening your understanding of every good thing we share for the sake of Christ" (Philemon v. 6 NIV). It is easy to douse the flames of

enthusiasm in others. All that needs to be done is to throw a little cold water of negativism on them. Too many have mastered the art of adding their two cents of negativity and discouragement to a situation. There is no shortage of pessimists out there. But a simple pat on the back, a word of affirmation, to someone can give them the aspiration and self-confidence to do amazing things. Those of us who build the most mutually beneficial and positive relationships with others are vulnerable enough to share those things nearest and dearest to their hearts. And nothing can be more valuable than a personal faith that produces an endless hope instead of a life philosophy offering nothing but an end void of any real hope. No wonder Paul challenged Philemon to aspire to share his winsome faith with others.

This was not some theoretical hypothesis on Paul's part. He was motivating Philemon to do what Paul did daily in his life. He was active in sharing his faith with everyone and everywhere. Can you imagine someone winning a million-dollar sweepstakes and never sharing the winnings with those closest to them? Is it possible to be connected to the Creator of the entire universe, to know Him through personal faith, and never be active in sharing the faith that brings forgiveness and eternal hope with

> Is it possible to be connected to the Creator of the entire universe and never be active in sharing the faith that brings forgiveness and eternal hope with others?

others? Paul's affirmation and encouragement to Philemon spurred him on, motivating him to aspire to share his own faith in his relationships with others. When our oldest daughter was young, we shared with her some good family news that we did not want anyone to know at the time. When we told her not to tell anyone, she replied, "But Daddy, what good is good news if you can't share it?" Out of the mouths of babes!

Jesus reminded His followers on more than one occasion that a truly wise person was one who not only knew what he should do but who put it into practice. A pat on the back will bring with it an aspiration to want to do something about it. It can challenge us to new beginnings. It will work in your business. It will work on your athletic team. It will work in the classroom. It will work in your church. It can work wonders in your home. Whenever we affirm someone, it can motivate them to try harder and to be better. This is why the most successful coaches are those who do not lead by intimidation and fear but by affirmation and encouragement. This is why the most successful businesses succeed over their competitors. This is why the

best educators are like Ava White, who recognized the importance of giving a young teenager a pat on the back, even when he might not have deserved it.

> The most successful coaches are those who do not lead by intimidation and fear but by affirmation and encouragement.

The first step in the development of positive, productive interpersonal relationships is the very principle Paul employed in the first paragraph of his letter to Philemon—a word of affirmation, a simple pat on the back. Someone you know needs a word like that from you today. Effective affirmation will always involve appreciation, authentication, and aspiration, and we can add to these a word about anticipation.

7 A WORD OF ANTICIPATION

*P*aul dropped a note of anticipation into the equation. He challenged Philemon to be active in sharing his faith so that he could become "effective" (Philemon v. 6). How? By "the acknowledgment of every good thing which is in you in Christ Jesus" (v. 6). There was something hidden behind this sentence. Remember that he was anticipating, in just a few more sentences, asking Philemon to receive Onesimus back. He was keenly aware that if Philemon possessed a full understanding of "every good thing" that was in him through Christ, he would have no recourse but to forgive and accept his rebellious runaway servant who was returning in genuine repentance. This sentence of Paul's letter is filled with *anticipation* that Philemon would, in fact, do the right thing. If Philemon came to this "acknowledgment of every good thing," it would include Christ's familiar command to forgive those who have wronged us.

Paul was anticipating that Philemon's "love . . . toward

all the saints" (v. 5) would include even the runaway and rebellious Onesimus, who had since come to faith. This would be a big pill to swallow. Perhaps only those who have been deeply wronged by someone held close and in confidence can know how difficult this might be. Paul had confidence in Philemon and anticipated a reconciliation as he penned these words. A few sentences later he would call upon his friend to "receive him [Onesimus] as you would me" (v. 17). And then Paul would continue by saying, "Having confidence in your obedience, I write to you, knowing that you will do even more than I say" (v. 21). If you are looking for a genuine pat on the back that is filled with the anticipation of a positive outcome, you need look no further than this epistle.

Paul was building positive relationships by maintaining an anticipation of the resolution of a broken relationship between two of his friends. And the key to this encouragement was in the fact that he was affirming both of them at the same time. He genuinely praised both Philemon and Onesimus in the same breath. There is a dynamic element in affirmation that leads us to aspire to do the right thing. Think about the last time you heard someone in your presence talk

> A simple pat on the back can have liberating effects.

positively about someone else. Most likely you went away feeling better about both individuals. A simple pat on the back can have liberating effects.

The problem with many of us who find ourselves in estranged relationships is that it seems easier to just walk away, resigned to the belief that we will go forward without any resolution leading to a reconciliation. If you are Onesimus, the offending party in a broken relationship, learn from him. First, get right in your relationship with yourself by getting right in your relationship with God, and then begin to anticipate the possibility of reconciliation through your own repentance, and possibly even restitution. If you are Philemon, the offended party, receive your Onesimus and forgive him when, and if, he returns in genuine remorse and repentance.

> Get right in your relationship with yourself by getting right in your relationship with God.

It might well be that there is an Onesimus in your life who has wronged you. Or, if you are honest, there may be a Philemon in your life who feels wronged by you. It might even be that you can identify with Paul, and you may be the one helping two friends mend a relationship. Often situations appear so complex that we do not know where to begin or how to get started. The place to start is the very place where Paul started—with a pat on the back, a word of affirmation. Imagine how Onesimus must have felt when he heard Paul say to Philemon, "If he has wronged you or owes anything, put that on my account" (v. 18). That affirmation spurred him to go home and make his wrong right. Imagine how Philemon felt when he read Paul's words: "Having confidence in your obedience, I write to you, knowing that you will do even more than I say" (v. 21). That was all the encouragement he would need to know that it is never wrong to do right.

Anticipation of reconciliation and reunion—it is the outcome of expressions of genuine affirmation.

8   A WORD OF ADMIRATION

*A*s Philemon continued to read this letter from Paul, he now came to some of the most beautiful words of admiration he could have received: "We have great joy and consolation in your love, because the hearts of the saints have been refreshed by you, brother" (Philemon v. 7). It was not just Philemon's love for Paul that brought him so much encouragement, but it was the fact that this love spread to "all the saints" (v. 5). It was Philemon's heart of love that was so admirable to the great apostle. This love that originated in his faith toward the Lord Jesus (v. 5), his eternal connection. This was what inspired his love for others. His genuine love for other people was what cheered and challenged, motivated and moved others to greater service and what brightened Paul's day miles across the Aegean Sea and all the way into the damp and dark prison cell where Paul was incarcerated. This warm and wonderful character trait of Philemon was what led Paul to declare that it was Philemon's love that gave Paul great hope and encouragement, for it refreshed the hearts of the saints everywhere.

Many years ago my wife, Susie, and I were guests of friends at Skibo Castle, outside Dornoch in the Scottish Highlands. Skibo was the former home of the late, great Scottish-American industrialist Andrew Carnegie. I was particularly fascinated by Carnegie's library, which was still in place as he had left it, filled with personal items and correspondence. His hunting log was still on his desk, bearing in their own handwriting the names Booker T. Washington and many other famous people from yesteryear. I came across the name of Charles Schwab. I suppose that every motivational speaker or writer from Norman Vincent Peale to Zig Ziglar has told his story at one time or another.

Charles Schwab worked for Carnegie. Schwab was among the first to earn a million dollars in a single calendar year. An initial response might assume that he knew more about the manufacturing of steel than anyone else in the world. But by his own admission, he knew little about that, and many others in the employ of Carnegie had far greater technical knowledge than he did. Why, then, would Carnegie elevate Schwab to the top of his organizational chart and pay him the handsome sum of a million

dollars a year? And keep in mind, this was shortly after the turn of the twentieth century and in a day when a million dollars was far more than it would be today. Schwab was Carnegie's man because of his unique ability to motivate others into productive relationships, which manifested in positive results. He was one of the first widely recognized motivators and movers of people.

Dale Carnegie, in his 1936 classic *How to Win Friends and Influence People*, quotes Schwab about his secret: "I consider my ability to arouse enthusiasm among my people the greatest asset I possess, and the way to develop the best that is in a person is by appreciation and encouragement. There is nothing else that so kills the ambition of a person as criticisms from superiors. I never criticize anyone. I believe in giving a person incentive to work. So I am anxious to praise but loath to find fault."[1]

Schwab let others know what he liked about them and then positively motivated them to build the most successful industry in the entire world. Many centuries before Schwab helped Carnegie build his financial dynasty through admiration and encouragement, Paul effectively used the same principles in this ancient piece of personal and private correspondence to his friend, Philemon. And, I might add, this still works today. The best way to increase

production and get positive results is still through appreciation, admiration, and affirmation . . . a simple pat on the back.

The best way to reach out and give someone a pat on the back is with a positive word of encouragement. Try it the next time you are standing in an office elevator, delayed at an airline counter, or conversing with a favorite server at your local restaurant. We will touch the lives of people today, many of whom have not heard a positive word of affirmation or admiration from anyone in years. Perhaps some for a lifetime. Some people go months, maybe years, without a personal word of admiration directed to their spouse and then wonder why the relationship has lost its spark. Some parents allow their teenagers to graduate from high school and move away without any remembrance of a word of affirmation or encouragement from a mom or a dad. A simple pat on the back can change someone's entire day and, in some cases, even the way they think about themselves. It can make work more productive, make the home more respectful and loving, and move your friends to enjoy your company and look forward to being in your presence.

> The best way to reach out and give someone a pat on the back is with a positive word of encouragement.

Some people today would find it difficult to say what Paul said to Philemon: that your love has given me great hope and encouragement, for you, brother, have refreshed the hearts of the saints. When our daughter, Holly, was in high school, one day I drove her to a basketball tournament being played at Saint Thomas Aquinas High School in Fort Lauderdale. Never having been on that campus before, I noticed a large sign on the football stadium that read Brian Piccolo Field. Brian was a hometown boy who played football there over a generation ago. He went on to enjoy a stellar college career at Wake Forest and then to the world-famous Chicago Bears of the NFL.

Alan McGinnis told his story in his book *The Friendship Factor*. On road trips, Piccolo's roommate with the Bears was the legendary African American running back Gale Sayers. In those early days of integration and racial strife in the 1960s, neither of them had ever had a close friend of the opposite race. Their love for each other and their friendship developed into one known far and wide and was immortalized in the motion picture titled *Brian's Song*.

During the 1969 season, Piccolo was diagnosed with cancer. He and Sayers had planned to sit together with their wives at the Professional Football Writers of America's

annual dinner in New York City, where Sayers was to receive the prestigious George Halas Award, given to the most courageous player, coach, or staff member in the NFL. Confined to what became his deathbed, Piccolo did not make the dinner. With tears streaming from his eyes and cascading down his cheeks, Sayers received the award, saying, "You flatter me by giving me this award. But I tell you here and now that I accept it for Brian Piccolo. Brian Piccolo is the man of courage who should receive this award. I love Brian Piccolo."[2] Seldom do we hear men express their admiration for one another publicly. We all need to know we are loved by someone . . . somewhere. The greatest motivational book ever written, the Bible, reminds us that "Love never fails" (1 Corinthians 13:8).

> We all need to know we are loved by someone . . . somewhere.

If there is someone in your circle of friends whose love has given you great joy and encouragement, why not learn from Paul and go ahead and let them know it? Sit down. Write a note of admiration. Give that someone a pat on the back. Most likely, it will do more for you than it will for them. Nothing opens the door to positive, productive interpersonal relationships more than words of admiration and affirmation.

9 A WORD OF AFFIRMATION

*C*ontinuing with Paul's letter to Philemon, the first paragraph concluded with a word of affirmation. Paul wrote that Philemon had "refreshed the hearts of the Lord's people" (Philemon v. 7 NIV). This was Paul's way of telling Philemon that he found it refreshing to be in his presence and to be the recipient of his words of encouragement. This word *refresh* in Paul's letter, written in Greek, carried with it the connotation of being relieved from pain. It is like a toothache that, after attention from a dentist, gets resolved, and the pain is relieved. What a feeling of refreshment. I have known people in my own experience who have been the embodiment of this word. Just being in their presence is a refreshing experience. My late friend Gene Whiddon had this effect on everyone he met. When he died a premature death, thousands of people from all walks of life filed by his casket. Each had a story to tell of how Gene had refreshed their lives through affirmation and encouragement.

How would you feel if you got a letter today from someone who said, "Your love has given me great hope and encouragement because you have refreshed the hearts of the saints"? You would sit up, eager to read what was coming next. In stark contrast, when we receive letters with words of caustic criticism in the first paragraph, we don't want to read further. During a sermon series I was preaching on this very subject from Philemon, there came a day when I received several letters in the mail. I opened the first one, and it blasted and blistered me and did so extremely unjustly. It wounded me greatly. The next several letters were filled with encouragement and affirmation. One writer wrote that from my recent sermon she had gained the encouragement needed to seek to mend the relationship with her estranged husband. Others told of miracles that had taken place in relationships when they put in place these principles of affirmation. Needless to say, words of affirmation go a long way in refreshing the hearts of those who receive them. We can keep going and keep doing what is right on the wings of one great compliment.

> We can keep going and keep doing what is right on the wings of one great compliment.

As I sit this afternoon in front of my computer screen

typing these words, an experience from my boyhood days has come racing through my mind. As a kid I played Little League baseball, and during my first two seasons, our coach was a big, husky, rough-and-tough man. He demanded perfection that ten-year-olds could not deliver. We were all intimidated by him and had very average seasons. But for my third and last year on the team, a new coach took over. I will never forget the team meeting he called after our first game. He called me up to his side and said to the group, "Did you boys see what Hawkins did last night? Instead of throwing home, where we had little chance to get the runner out, he faked the throw, threw to second, and caught the runner off guard and got us out of the inning. Now that is what I want all of us to do: to think, to anticipate the play." And then, with a pat on my back, he said, "Great job." He affirmed me in front of everyone. He believed in me and let me know it. I can't tell you what that word of affirmation did for me. I played that season over my head, won the batting title, and made the All-Star team. (Unfortunately, that was the apex of my entire athletic career!) Never underestimate the power of positive affirmation in your relationships.

The greatest affirmer who ever lived was the Lord Jesus Christ. This was one of the reasons so many people flocked to Him. The religious zealots of His day were uncomfortable around Him. But the people were refreshed by being in His presence. He simply walked around the shores of Galilee and the dusty paths of Judea affirming others, giving them constant words of encouragement. One day in the village of Bethany, a woman came to Him and anointed His feet with very expensive perfume that cost the equivalent of an entire year's salary in the first-century world. Several of the disciples began to rebuke her, considering it a waste and saying she should have sold it and given the money to the poor. Imagine how that woman must have felt when Jesus looked into her eyes and said, "She has done a beautiful thing to me" (Matthew 26:10 NIV).

> The greatest affirmer who ever lived was the Lord Jesus Christ. This was one of the reasons so many people flocked to Him.

And what about the woman who was taken in the very act of adultery? The religious leaders of the day surrounded her with their long, pointed fingers of accusation as they prepared to execute their judgment on her by stoning. How she must have felt when Jesus rebuked them and, looking straight into her repentant heart, said, "Neither do I condemn you; go and sin no more" (John 8:11). It might well

have been the first time in her entire life that anyone had given her a word of affirmation. It likely transformed the way she thought about herself and changed her entire life.

Who of us has not put ourselves in the place of the big fisherman Simon Peter? He blew it for sure. So self-confident and full of braggadocio, but when the chips were down, he wimped out and failed miserably, denying repeatedly that he ever knew our Lord. How he must have felt a few days later when he ate along the shore of Galilee with the resurrected Christ, who let him know that one failure did not make a flop (John 21). Peter was never the same again and went from that word of affirmation to become the undisputed leader of first-generation Christianity. Never underestimate how a simple pat on the back, a word of affirmation, can refresh the hearts of the saints.

10 A WORD OF APPLICATION

*L*ook around you today. As I mentioned earlier, there most likely are people in your world who have lived months, perhaps years, without anyone, anywhere, at any time affirming them. Although they may never articulate it, they are looking for it, longing for it. Instead of saying, "I wish someone would affirm me today," begin looking for someone you can affirm, and watch the biblical principle of reaping and sowing come into effect. Someone you know just might be hanging by a thread with hope almost gone. It just may be that if you don't reach out to them with a word of hope and encouragement, no one else in their entire world ever will. The problem in so many interpersonal relationships is found in the fact that many of us are simply reactive and too few of us are proactive in this area. The very ones we are hoping will affirm us just might be the very ones hoping we will affirm them. Be proactive. Take the initiative. Do something. Reach out to that someone.

The absolute master in the art of affirmation was the Lord Jesus Christ. He went about His world lifting people up. Once in the middle of a hot day, He met a woman at a well. Everyone in her village had criticized her. But He reached over with a figurative pat on the back and told her of the living water He provided, which in her would be a "fountain of water springing up into everlasting life" (John 4:14). That simple one-on-one encounter became the catalyst that brought her entire village to faith in Him (John 4). One day on a Roman cross of execution, He turned to the man hanging on the cross next to Him. Through parched lips, Jesus reached out in His own darkest hour with words of hope and affirmation: "Today you will be with Me in Paradise" (Luke 23:43). Not long after that, He took that man by His own nail-pierced hand and walked into heaven with him.

> Through parched lips, Jesus reached out in His own darkest hour with words of hope and affirmation: "Today you will be with Me in Paradise" (Luke 23:43).

Back to Philemon as he read the letter from Paul. The opening paragraph explodes with affirmation wrapped in a word of appreciation. There was authentication. This was not some cleverly devised manipulative maneuver. It was from the heart. There was also a note of aspiration in this paragraph. Paul was challenging his friend to aspire to be proactive in his relationship with Onesimus. And there was a note of anticipation. It served to get Philemon into the proper mindset to anticipate a mutually beneficial relationship to come about. Paul also left a note of admiration, assuring Philemon that he genuinely admired his love, and it was a source of joy and encouragement. Finally, it was all topped off with affirmation. As Philemon progressed through these sentences, he must have sat up a little straighter in his chair and felt better about himself with each passing phrase. I am confident you or I would feel the same way if we received such a letter from someone we loved and respected as much as Philemon did Paul.

Everything has a beginning, and new beginnings are of vital importance. Many relationships that "might have been" crashed and burned on takeoff because they did not get started right. The very best place to begin a positive relationship is with a sincere pat on the back.

Now is the time to make a conscious decision to put this principle into practice. The Code Series of devotionals now includes over a dozen offerings. I would rather have my readers "do" one chapter than read a hundred of them. Affirmation must be authentic. To be effective, a pat on the back must incorporate some practical principles.

1. Make it *personal.* Paul did. He did not send out a word of affirmation to Philemon through a third party. He did so in an intensely personal piece of private correspondence. Affirmations can lose their positive effectiveness when we ask someone to tell someone else something for us. In short, do it yourself.

2. Make it *positive.* Affirmations lose their value unless they are delivered in a positive vein. The best attempt some make at affirmation is to say something like "Well, you did the best you could, and I suppose that is above average." That is not much of a pat on the back. Make it personal, and make sure it is positive.

3. Make it *present.* Paul wrote this letter in the present tense. He told Philemon, "I hear about [you] . . ." (v. 5 NIV). True affirmation needs to be up-to-date and prompt to be effective. It rings a bit hollow and doesn't mean much to affirm someone now for something they may have done ten years ago. Make it present, fresh, and current.

4. Make it *pointed.* Paul was specific and pointed in his affirmation of Philemon. General affirmations like "You are a great guy" do not go very far. We

must be pointed in our praise of others. Let the other party know specifically why it is you are giving them a pat on the back. Spell it out.

5. Make it *plain*. Philemon had no trouble at all understanding what Paul was saying. It was plain. It was not garbled or couched in any type of linguistic gymnastics. We often try to excuse ourselves, saying, "Oh, he knows I appreciate him." Are you sure? Tell your friend so with a personal, positive, present, pointed, and plain word of affirmation.

6. Make it *passionate*. Like Paul's words to Philemon, your affirmation should issue out of your heart. Paul mentioned that Philemon's love had "refreshed the hearts" of others (v. 7 NIV). Phony affirmations are quickly exposed and accomplish nothing. Make sure your pat on the back is from the heart, and make it passionate. Interested in building positive and productive relationships? Then begin, as Paul did to Philemon, with a genuine pat on the back.

PART 3

THE WIN-WIN PRINCIPLE

Though I might be very bold in Christ to command you what is fitting, yet for love's sake I rather appeal to you— being such a one as Paul, the aged, and now also a prisoner of Jesus Christ—I appeal to you for my son Onesimus, whom I have begotten while in my chains, who once was unprofitable to you, but now is profitable to you and to me.

—PHILEMON VV. 8–11

$\mathscr{A}$fter beginning with the important place that affirmation plays in relationships, Paul then turned to what can be described as the win-win principle. This concept was made popular by Stephen Covey in his blockbuster bestseller *The Seven Habits of Highly Effective People.* But long before Covey wrote on the subject, Paul had already perfected it. In verses 8–11, Paul was appealing

to Philemon to see how they all can come out winners in this relationship.

Some relationships are built on competition. These fall into the category of win-lose relationships. That is, some will only stay in a relationship in which they always win and the other person always loses. They feel they always have to take center stage, win every argument, and be in control. In fact, it is not enough that they always have to win; they are not content unless the other party always loses.

These types of relationships, built on competition, never win in the long run because everyone ends up losing. Take, for example, a husband and a wife. He constantly orders her around the house. He coerces and controls. After a while, her resentment is sure to build. For years he thinks he is winning. But one day he wakes up to see she has had enough and is gone. And in the end, they both end up losing. This also can happen with parent-and-child relationships, when a parent thinks he or she has to win every argument, keep a thumb on the kid, and control them by withholding the use of the car. The child leaves home one day and seldom returns, and they all end up in the loss column.

Those who play the game of relationships in a spirit

of competition—the win-lose principle—never are real winners in the long run. When the final whistle blows, everyone ends up losing.

Some relationships are built on compromise. This can be referred to as the lose-win relationship. Some people have such low feelings of self-worth that they feel the only way they can maintain a relationship is to always let the other party win and sacrifice their own desires, hoping that, in turn, they will be accepted. They think by allowing the other party to win every argument and dominate every situation, this will somehow help them maintain the relationship.

Relationships built on compromise, like those built on competition, produce little, if any, long-term positive results. In the end, both parties end up losing. It is difficult over time to maintain respect for someone who plays the relationship game in the lose-win arena.

> It is difficult over time to maintain respect for someone who plays the relationship game in the lose-win arena.

Other relationships are built on complacency. These can be referred to as lose-lose relationships. These people are really more interested in seeing the other lose than in seeing themselves win. Misery, for some, loves company. This

type of individual is complacent, never putting much into a relationship and never expecting much in return. Those who play the game like this lose in life and will stay in a relationship as long as the other party is losing as well. But as soon as some good fortune may come to the other party, they usually go on their way. Sadly, some people have lost in life and have such a low level of self-confidence that they find a comfort level in lose-lose relationships.

Like the other relationships already mentioned, with those who play lose-lose, everyone ends up losing. Complacency sets in and produces no real winners in relationships.

Then there are those relationships built on capitulation. Having no relational resilience, these people simply quit. When things don't go their way, they just pick up their ball and go home. We all know people who get started and then stop. They have been involved in one relationship after another, and every new one is "the right one." But after a short while, it is over, and on to the next. For some, it seems easier to just walk away and move on to what is next. Like those who play lose-win, relationships based on capitulation never produce any results. The reason is obvious: everyone ends up losing.

Another way some people play the relationship game is

on the field of cancellation. These people never actually get in the game because they forfeit before the first whistle ever blows. For whatever reason, they never make the slightest effort in a relationship. It is impossible to sustain a relationship that never really got started in the first place. Sadly, through this type of passivity, others are kept from mutually beneficial relationships that might have been.

There is a better way to begin and sustain positive relationships. Those who play by the win-win principle find cooperation. Win-win relationships are always mutually beneficial. This person is wise enough to know that if the other party in the relationship wins, he or she ends up winning as well. Or, as Paul said to Philemon, Onesimus "now is profitable to you and to me" (v. 11).

> Those who play by the win-win principle find cooperation. Win-win relationships are always mutually beneficial.

The wise husband always seeks what is best for his wife and knows that when she wins, he wins as well. A mom always wants what is best for her child. At the office, wise managers know that if the company helps the customers win, they can stay in business. The most productive relationships in life are built on cooperation, the win-win principle.

Relationships built on competition (win-lose) do not get very far before they disintegrate. Zacchaeus tried to play this game. Most of us remember his story. He ripped off others and played win-lose with many of the people in Jericho. But one day he saw the light, embraced a win-win attitude, restored what he had cheated from others, and ended up being the most popular person at the party (Luke 19:1–10).

Relationships built on compromise (lose-win) don't get very far either. The woman of Sychar played this game. She possessed such low self-esteem that she felt the only way to get any attention was to play in the loser's bracket, allowing the men of the town to win by using her. But one day she met a Man at a well and learned how to play win-win. She went back to those very people and introduced them to this One who had changed the way she thought about herself. And everyone in Sychar ended up winning (John 4).

The dying thief spent his life playing on the field of complacency (lose-lose). Talk about a guy who had lost in life and waited until it was almost too late. But nailed to a Roman cross, he connected with his Maker, who hung on a middle cross next to him, and they both ended up on the winning team (Luke 23:43).

Elijah capitulated. After winning the big prize on Mount Carmel, the next day an interpersonal relationship

spat with a queen named Jezebel sent him on a journey of capitulation that ended with him in a cave contemplating suicide (1 Kings 19).

The point is, no matter how you have fared in relationships across the years, you can get on a winning team today. Jesus of Nazareth was not just some musty-smelling character from bygone days, a figment of someone's imagination, who is totally irrelevant in our twenty-first-century world. He is alive and can do for us what He did for so many in the Gospels. He walked around, lifting people out of their losing ways and putting them in win-win relationships with Himself. Paul found himself on Jesus' team and passed the ball to Philemon—and to us.

> Jesus of Nazareth was not just some musty-smelling character from bygone days. He is alive and can do for us what He did for so many in the Gospels.

Now, how do we get in the game ourselves? In Paul's letter to Philemon, he revealed four critical steps to the win-win principle of relationships. Step one: be sensitive. Step two: be submissive. Step three: be supportive. And step four: be sensible. It is time now not only to turn the page to the next chapter, but to turn the page in the book of your life to the next chapter of positive and productive interpersonal relationships.

11   BE SENSITIVE

*S*ensitivity is essential in the building of worthwhile relationships. When Paul said to Philemon, "Therefore, though I might be very bold in Christ to command you what is fitting" (Philemon v. 8), he was essentially saying, "I could be bold and order you do the right thing." But this people person was sensitive to the fact that people do not like to be bullied through coercion or compulsion. The best way to win them is through consideration and cooperation. Paul could have played the win-lose game, but he resisted that temptation. His desire was that all three of these men would emerge as winners when all was said and done.

Instead of being sensitive in relationships, there are some who like to give orders and make other people squirm. Some are foolish enough to think they win by taking this approach. The easy thing for Paul to do with Philemon was to call in his chips and order Philemon to do what he ought to do. But Paul resisted. There was no hint of a command. In fact, he appealed to Philemon on the basis of love and with a high degree of sensitivity, saying, "For love's sake I rather appeal to you" (v. 9). Any other approach would have caused guilt or a grudge, with a damaging result to all three of the relationships.

When *sensitivity* becomes a lost word in our relational vocabulary, we have eyes for our side of the issue only. Paul was extremely sensitive to Philemon here. His goal was a long-term, continuous relationship with his trusted friend. Consequently, he was sensitive enough to realize that if he muscled and maneuvered his way into this breach, both Philemon and Onesimus would end up losing in the end.

> When *sensitivity* becomes a lost word in our relational vocabulary, we have eyes for our side of the issue only.

The fact that Paul reminded Philemon that he could pull rank in the issue was not lost in his sensitivity to the delicate matter, which he would soon broach—that being, to receive Onesimus back, and not as just a servant but as a "beloved brother" (v. 16).

Paul had already encouraged Onesimus, the offending party, to do what he ought to do. This meant to face up to his wrong and go back to Philemon in a spirit of general remorse and repentance, making restitution and asking for

forgiveness. Next, Paul turned to Philemon, the offended party, encouraging him to do what he ought to do. This meant to forgive and receive the repentant Onesimus "no longer as a slave but more than a slave—a beloved brother" (v. 16).

How many relational breaches would be resolved if we would simply do what we ought to do? At home. In the office. In our social circles. The first step in developing relationships in which everyone involved ends up winning is to be sensitive, to walk in the other person's shoes for a while.

Some people live a lifetime with few long-term, lasting interpersonal relationships because of their desire to control and command others on their own terms. The lack of any semblance of sensitivity to the others' feelings and needs is too often prevalent for many of us. If you are in a relationship with someone who always has to be in control, who issues commands with no sensitivity to your own needs, you are headed for trouble, no matter how much you continue to live in denial.

> If you are in a relationship with someone who always has to be in control, you are headed for trouble, no matter how much you continue to live in denial.

The first step in paving the way

for win-win relationships that are genuinely, mutually beneficial is to be sensitive. It may take two to tango, but often in relationships one person doing what he or she ought to do—being sensitive to the other's needs—can start a new beginning in which everyone ends up on the winning team. Be sensitive.

12   BE SUBMISSIVE

A submissive spirit and attitude are indispensable to all worthwhile relationships. Paul continued his demonstration of the importance of building win-win relationships by informing Philemon that his appeal was on the basis of love: "Yet for love's sake I rather appeal to you—being such a one as Paul, the aged, and now also a prisoner of Jesus Christ" (Philemon v. 9). Love always seeks the other's highest good. Love is always equated with action in the Bible. While Paul could have exerted his apostolic authority or appealed on the basis of his elder statesmanship, directing Philemon in the process, he was sensitive and submissive enough to choose the path of love. Seeing the end from the beginning, he was wise enough to know that lasting relationships are never built on competition—the win-lose approach—but on the basis of love, resulting in a place where everyone involved can claim victory.

Writing in Greek, Paul chose a strong word that we

translate into the English word *appeal*. Appearing more than a hundred times in the New Testament, it is often translated as "plead," "strongly urge," or "encourage." Paul was not barking out orders like some boot camp drill sergeant. He was asking, appealing, pleading, urging, encouraging Philemon. He was sensitive to the situation and submissive in his approach to bring reconciliation to the relationship.

In our own efforts to mend relationships, win friends, or influence others, the manner in which we make our appeal is of utmost importance. How do we go about winning others to our persuasion? Some of us waste valuable time appealing to others strictly on the basis of reason. Others make their appeals on the basis of merit, who they are or where they may be coming from. Still others appeal on the basis of such things as tenure, seeking to convince others that they have earned the right to make their case because of their experience. Paul could have appealed to Philemon on the basis of each of these, but he instead chose love. And when he wrote that he was appealing on the basis of love, he chose the highest level of love, *agape* love, as he penned these words. This type of love is best defined as "no matter what someone may do to you by insult or injury, you seek for them only their highest good." This is

God's love. This is submissive love that seeks the other's best interest. It is the win-win type of love.

This is the very type of love that epitomizes Jesus of Nazareth. He could have played win-lose with all of us. He could have ordered us to obey Him. He could pull our strings like a puppeteer to force us to fall in step and love Him. But what did He do? What does He still do? He appealed to us on the basis of love. In fact, in the Bible's attempt to define Him, it simply says, "God is love" (1 John 4:16). When demonstrated in a win-win fashion, this type of love breaks down barriers and cements relationships. There can be no long-term, constructive, interpersonal relationships without being based on the appeal of love.

> There can be no long-term, constructive, interpersonal relationships without being based on the appeal of love.

Think about it: Which motivates you and appeals to you the most—an order or an appeal? Imagine a mother saying to her daughter, "I am telling you right now to get your grades up. That is an order. You have no choice." What real motivation do you think this type of order has on a young person? How much better it is when parents make appeals based on love, resulting in win-win outcomes. How many homes have been lost because a husband or a wife played only the win-lose scenario in their relationships? Those who are sensitive and appeal on the basis of love with a submissive spirit are the ones who make it to the finish line.

Love has its own way of finding out what is right and doing it. Love is not a passive noun. It always is equated with action. Love is something we do! "For God so loved the world" that He did something about it; He "gave His only begotten Son" (John 3:16). When, in our relationships, we submit to love, we end up doing what we ought to do much more quickly and completely than when someone seeks to coerce or command us against our volition. Cognizant of this, Paul was both sensitive and submissive in appealing to Philemon on the basis of love.

This is a worthy model for us. We can excel ourselves and motivate others in the process if we stop insisting on our own way by becoming more sensitive and submissive in our relationships with others. There would be more harmony in the home and more order in the office if more of us would stop trying to control and coerce each other and take a page from Paul by appealing to one another on the basis of love. Being sensitive and submissive are the first steps in producing win-win relationships that are positive and productive. Be submissive.

13   BE SUPPORTIVE

*M*utual support is an essential element in the building of lasting friendships. Paul continued on the playing field of win-win relationships by saying, "I appeal to you for my son Onesimus, whom I have begotten while in my chains, who was once unprofitable to you, but now is profitable to you and to me" (Philemon vv. 10–11). Win-win relationships are characterized by a bonding, a sense of mutual support. Having someone's back, taking up for them verbally, is a part of the cement that holds a friendship together. It is the win-win principle in action.

Paul referred to this runaway slave as his "son" (v. 10). And in so doing, he was expressing to Philemon his unqualified support of Onesimus. He chose a Greek word that is a term of endearment—with the connotation of not just a son but a small child. By this choice of word, Paul was informing Philemon that Onesimus, who was already on his way home, was still young in the faith, trying to do the right thing, and in need of support and love.

Paul was halfway through his letter and now getting to the point. Remember, verse 10 is the first mention of Onesimus in the entire letter. Can you picture the wealthy aristocrat, Philemon, receiving a letter from Paul? He must have been so anxious to read it, and as he began, Paul affirmed him with a pat on the back. By this point I imagine that Philemon was sitting up a little straighter in his chair, smiling and feeling pretty good about himself. And then a name appeared, embedded in the middle of a paragraph, and leaped off the page at him. *Onesimus! That scoundrel.* Philemon must have felt like most of us would have felt if someone we knew and in whom we had placed our trust embezzled money from us, left town, and was never heard from again. But wait. Read this line again— "my son Onesimus." The letter continued, he "became my son while I was in chains" (v. 10 NIV). Philemon must have thought he was dreaming. This was either the world's biggest coincidence, or it was the hand of God at work in these three relationships.

Do you see what was unfolding? A broken relationship was about to be mended, and Paul, the catalyst, was not only being sensitive to the situation but supportive as well. Previously in his letter he had expressed his support of Philemon by letting him know that his love had

given Paul great hope and encouragement, and Philemon had refreshed the hearts of the saints (v. 7). Then he let Philemon know that he supported Onesimus in the same way he did Philemon. Paul had shared the gospel with Onesimus when they were cellmates in a Roman prison and was there when Onesimus was born again to faith in Jesus Christ. He had become Paul's own son in the faith, and now, like any good and godly father, Paul supported Onesimus in his new faith journey.

Cooperation, the win-win principle, is the best way to develop lasting relationships. You know you have a true friend when they are not simply sensitive to your feelings but are supportive of you in front of others. Think about your own relationships. Do your friends see you as one who is as sensitive to their needs as you are to your own? Or would they say you too often think only of yourself and how the relationship can benefit you? Do those in your inner circle of relationships think of you as being submissive? Or do you generally insist on getting your own way in order to relate and be happy? Do they have the assurance that you will be supportive of them when issues

> You know you have a true friend when they are not simply sensitive to your feelings but are supportive of you in front of others.

might arise? Do they know, without a shadow of a doubt, that you would rise to their defense if the situation called for it?

It is not too late to get in the game of win-win relationships. Step one: start being more sensitive to other people's needs and feelings. Step two: stop insisting on your own way all the time and, like Christ, develop a sense of submission. And step three: start being supportive by letting others know, as Paul did to Philemon, that you are a person who can be trusted to rise to a friend's defense when the need arises. Win-win relationships involve one final step: simply being sensible, using good old common sense.

14   BE SENSIBLE

*F*aith is the essence of the Christian life. In some ways, it can be referred to as uncommon sense. Often when common sense says the situation is hopeless, we need the uncommon sense to believe that God can still make the impossible possible. As Paul came to this part of his letter, he was appealing to Philemon to be sensible, to use some good old common sense in the matter:

> Who [Onesimus] once was unprofitable to you, but now is profitable to you and to me. I am sending him back. You therefore receive him, that is, my own heart, whom I wished to keep with me, that on your behalf he might minister to me in my chains for the gospel. But without your consent I wanted to do nothing, that your good deed might not be by compulsion, as it were, but voluntary. For perhaps he departed for a while for this purpose, that you might receive him forever, no longer as a slave but more than a slave—a beloved brother, especially to me but

how much more to you, both in the flesh and in the Lord. (Philemon vv. 11–16)

Paul said that Onesimus once was useless to Philemon but now he was useful to both Philemon and him. This was the heart of the letter, the point of the win-win principle. When the other party in a relationship wins, you win also. One of the reasons so many relationships fail is that we are simply not using common sense and being sensible about matters. Some still think that the only profitable way to be in a relationship is to play the game of life on the field of win-lose relationships where they win all the time. Paul was showing that there is a much better way.

> One of the reasons so many relationships fail is that we are simply not using common sense and being sensible about matters.

Paul referred to Onesimus as previously being "unprofitable" (v. 11). Now, that was an understatement. Remember, this was the same guy who had ripped Philemon off and then ran away. Then on the heels of this honest confession, Paul wrote two words that turned the whole context of the letter: *but now*! I love those two monosyllabic words, "but now." There was no attempt to justify Onesimus's previous

actions. Quite the contrary, Paul readily admitted that he was before "unprofitable," useless. But he didn't leave it there. He continued, "But now [Onesimus] is profitable to you and to me" (v. 11). It can be a win-win situation for all involved. When people like Onesimus become connected at the source and come into a vital personal relationship with Jesus Christ, this does not produce some nebulous, inefficient, ineffective, useless person. It produces people who are useful and profitable for the kingdom and the sake of the gospel to everyone with whom they come into contact.

Be sensible. This is a good time for a bit of a warning. Some can often mistake a win-win relationship for a win-lose relationship if they look only at the moment. For example, think about the parent-child relationship. Often when a loving parent executes discipline upon a child, the child thinks only in the short term and therefore confuses the relationship for one of win-lose, in which the parent is winning and the child is losing. But the wise parent is sensible and thinking long-term, not trying to pull rank on the kid, but ultimately building a win-win relationship that will last over time. Loving parents have their child's end in mind (no pun intended). In the end they desire to see their child move through life with a healthy respect for

authority and become a better and more productive person because of it. What the child might view as a win-lose scenario is in actuality a win-win. But we must be sensible to see it.

This principle plays out in every field of life and not just the home. In the office, employees can sometimes see the boss's intensity as a win-lose affair, though, in fact, he or she may be striving for a situation in which everyone ends up winning. Effective leaders motivate their people to produce more, and in so doing, the company stays in business, employees keep their jobs, and the customers receive value and service. The same principle plays out on every athletic field on every school campus. The effective coach may appear to be hard-driving and commanding when all the while his or her motivation is to produce winners, not just on the field but in life as well. Being sensible, just using some common sense, is a vital ingredient in the building of positive, productive interpersonal relationships.

Now, how does this practically work out? We must have the common sense to see that in win-lose relationships, both parties end up losing. There are no real winners. However,

> We must have the common sense to see that in win-lose relationships, both parties end up losing.

when we begin to apply the win-win principle, there are no losers. Everyone ends up winners. This is true in both of the great laboratories of life—marriage and management, the home and the office.

Remember the scenario in which the husband and wife are in a win-lose relationship? He orders her around. He controls her. He barks out his commands. Eventually, there will come a day when her resentment reaches a boiling point. He thinks he has been winning all this time. But she finally finds the courage to walk out the door and never returns. And in the end, they both lose. There are no eventual winners in this type of relationship.

In contrast, imagine another husband who is always sensitive to his wife's needs. He realizes the biblical principle of mutual submission. He appeals to her on the basis of love and expresses such continuous support of her that she never has to wonder if he would come to her defense should the need ever arise. How do you think a wife would respond to a husband like that? She would have no problem submitting to a love like that, which always has her best interests in mind. He wins. She wins. And they live happily ever after.

The same sensible principle works with parents and children. Consider a dad who plays win-lose with his son.

He has to win every single argument. He is right every single time. He barks orders to his son, often in the presence of the son's friends. He completely seeks to control his life in every way. He keeps his thumb on him and uses power to get his way. All the while he thinks he is winning. But resentment builds, and there comes a day when the son leaves home for college. And he leaves home, all right—seldom to return and never to call. A dad loses a son's love. A son loses a father's relationship. No one ends up winning.

How much better it is when a dad is sensitive, submissive, supportive, and sensible enough to discipline his son in love and keep the lines of communication open and clear along the way. They both end up winning and enjoying a lifetime of positive and productive fellowship.

The win-win principle that is good for family relationships is also good for the workplace. Think about it. Here is a salesperson and a purchaser in a win-lose relationship. The seller of the product tries to always squeeze as much as she can and get an unfair edge without the buyer knowing it. She thinks she is winning. But after a while, profit margins shrink, the company goes out of business, and the salesperson loses a good account in the process. On the other hand, here is a sensible salesperson who plays

win-win. He is wise enough and has enough common sense to see that the other party stays in business by making a profit on their goods. He has a genuine interest in how their business is prospering and is smart enough to know he will keep a good account as long as his customer is thriving. He wins when they win. He keeps accounts when his customers stay in business. It is a win-win deal.

Be sensible. There is only one way to have sustained mutually beneficial relationships in life, and that is when everyone wins in the end.

15 AND THE RESULT?

$\mathcal{P}$aul reminded Philemon that Onesimus was now "profitable to you and to me" (Philemon v. 11). There you have it in a simple phrase. Two thousand years before modern leadership and relationship gurus ever talked the win-win principle, Paul was putting it into practice. Note the winners in this relationship. Did Paul win? Yes. He had the joy of being a channel of blessing in getting two men whom he personally led to faith in Christ, at different times, in different places, back together in a mended relationship. Had he resorted to ordering Philemon instead of appealing to him in love, it might never have happened. In the end, he could savor the love and support of both of his friends. He won.

Did Philemon win? Yes. He got Onesimus back, this time as a brother who was profitable and useful to him. And he received Onesimus's repentance and restitution along with him. Did Onesimus win? Yes. He got to go home. And what was more, he returned "no longer as

a slave" but as a "beloved brother" (v. 16). There are no losers when people learn to play win-win in their relationships. This secret to positive interpersonal relationships is obtained and maintained when we are sensitive, submissive, supportive, and sensible in our dealings with each other.

Pause just a minute to go back and remember the premise of the Connection Code. We will never properly relate to each other until we properly relate to ourselves, and we will never properly relate to ourselves until we properly relate to the Lord and find our self-worth in Him. There are a lot of people who think that when we put on the uniform of the Christian faith, we start playing on a losing team. Years ago Ted Turner, media mogul and baseball team owner, made headlines with his comment, "Christianity is a religion for losers."[3] There are a lot of people who go through life thinking that Christianity is about religion without ever discovering that it is all about relationships. Religion has a history of playing win-lose. It has coerced, controlled, oppressed, obsessed, and virtually enslaved people through the centuries. It has been at the root of world conflicts and today is the cause of so much tension and unrest in the Middle East.

Paul was not about religion. He was all about

relationships. And there is a world of difference. For Paul all meaningful relationships began by getting connected through faith to the Lord Jesus Christ. Jesus was never about religion. In fact, He openly and often rebuked

> Jesus was never about religion. He was, and still is, about relationships.

its excesses and perversions of God's original intent. He was, and still is, about relationships.

How does this eternal connection with Jesus Christ work out experientially? He plays win-win in His personal relationships with us. As with Paul's example, He is first of all sensitive. He never orders, compels, coerces, or commands us to relate positively to Him. He appeals to us on the basis of His love. Second, He is submissive. He submitted Himself to a vicious and vicarious execution in order to demonstrate His love and make a way out of no way for us. He is also supportive. He stands by our side and calls us His own children. He never leaves us or forsakes us. And when we are in a saving relationship with Him, one day He will stand by our side, as our advocate, supporting us before His Father's throne of judgment. Finally, Jesus is sensible. We should be too. It just makes sense to place our faith and trust in Him. And unless we do, we will never know how valuable we are,

nor will we ever sense our highest level of self-worth or self-love.

Let's recap with some practical pointers to remember. It is far better to put into practice the lessons of one chapter of a book than to simply read a hundred of them. We did not learn to ride a bicycle by reading a manual about it. We learned by climbing on and falling off a few times before we got the hang of it. The same holds true in our personal relationships. We have to be vulnerable and take risks to make them flourish. Let's climb on with these practical pointers:

1. *Be sensitive.* Try to put yourself in the other person's place. Seek to recognize their struggles and consider what they might be thinking. Be attuned to their needs. Don't try to bully them to your way of thinking by coercion, compulsion, or command. Win them through consideration and cooperation.

2. *Be submissive.* This does not mean you should become a doormat. But it never hurts to lose a few little battles in order to win a far bigger war. Resign yourself to the fact that you don't have to win every insignificant argument or point of contention. Begin to appeal to other people on the basis of love,

which seeks their own highest good. If they win, you win.

3. *Be supportive.* Let your friends know where you stand, and leave no doubt in their minds that when the chips are down, they can count on you and your support. Find someone who is down or has been wronged, and come to their aid with encouragement and support. They will never forget it.

4. *Be sensible.* Just use some good old common sense in your relationships. Get smart. When the other person in your relationship wins, you win with them. Leave behind, forever, the erroneous idea that not winning every single element of a relationship shows weakness. Wake up. Be sensible. Win-win is the only positive, productive way to play the game of relationships in life.

PART 4

BURYING THE HATCHET

I am sending him back. You therefore receive him, that is, my own heart, whom I wished to keep with me, that on your behalf he might minister to me in my chains for the gospel. But without your consent I wanted to do nothing, that your good deed might not be by compulsion, as it were, but voluntary. For perhaps he departed for a while for this purpose, that you might receive him forever, no longer as a slave but more than a slave—a beloved brother, especially to me but how much more to you, both in the flesh and in the Lord.

—PHILEMON VV. 12–16

*L*et's just bury the hatchet." How many times have we heard this well-worn phrase, and how few times have we genuinely put it into practice? It carries with it all the connotations of mending broken relationships,

forgetting old scores, and beginning again, afresh and anew. The phrase finds its origin in American Indian culture. When making peace with each other, they would ceremoniously bury a hatchet in the ground to signify those hostilities were over and done with. The capacity to forgive is one of the most vital, and often one of the most overlooked, concepts in ongoing interpersonal relationships. The ability to forgive others, and sometimes even ourselves, is essential in the maintenance of positive and mutually beneficial relationships.

The single most important factor in ongoing relationships is the ability to forgive, to bury the hatchet, when we have been wronged. Paul's letter to Philemon teaches us that positive relationships are not simply built on affirmation and accommodation, but their fabric must be woven with strands of forgiveness for them to endure. Any relationship that is lasting and worthwhile will have its moments of stress and disappointment, even brokenness, at times. The ability to forgive a wrong is always found in the most lasting relationships. In fact, the most secure ones are usually those in which people have weathered the storms and buried the hatchets.

> The single most important factor in ongoing relationships is the ability to forgive, to bury the hatchet, when we have been wronged.

My wife, Susie, and I have now been married over half a century. There have been times when I have been insensitive to her needs or spoken harshly. But she has always forgiven me and moved on. In raising our daughters, there were times we made mistakes and our patience ran thin. But our girls have always forgiven us. There were times when they did not always obey and later came to ask for forgiveness, and we always buried the hatchet with lessons learned and applied.

Unfortunately, many interpersonal relationships with so much potential are destroyed by a lack of forgiveness. When some cannot swallow their pride and bury the hatchet with another, they are building barriers in place of bridges to better relationships. Forgiveness, accompanied by the desire to move forward, is key to successful marriages, productive business ventures, continued local church health and growth, and lasting friendships.

In order to bury the hatchet in relationships, it is imperative to remember that there are two sides of a coin. As the old adage says, "It takes two to tango." There is an offending party and an offended party in broken relationships. And if we are honest, each of us has been both the offender and the offended. Onesimus was the offending party in this drama before us. He was a bond

servant to Philemon and under contractual obligations. Under the cover of night, Onesimus robbed Philemon and ran away. There is also an offended party in broken relationships. That is, there is one who has been wronged or wounded. The Bible makes plain that Philemon was the offended party. And the truth is, in most broken relationships, we need a "Paul," someone who can stand in the middle and help each party see the part they must play to make wrongs right again.

Two things must happen, one on the part of the offending party and the other on the part of the offended party, to genuinely mend a broken relationship. The offending party must come to the table with a repentant heart. If not, there can be no genuine reconciliation. If Onesimus had simply said he was sorry and returned with no recourse or change of heart or attitude, the wound would never have healed and the relationship would never have mended. How many times have we seen this scenario play out when the offending party is not truly sorry but simply sorry they got caught? There must be a truly repentant heart on the part of the offending party.

However, it takes two to bury the hatchet. There must be a receptive heart on the part of the offended party that is void of a spirit of resentment or retaliation. Most often the biggest burden falls on those who have been deeply wronged in a relationship. As a pastor for decades, I have noticed that most relationships are destroyed not because the offending party lacked a repentant heart but because the offended party would not receive the other, forgive, and move on. Both parties have a major role in seeing true reconciliation become a reality.

Most broken relationships can be salvaged. If I were speaking now, I would raise my voice a little here for emphasis. *"Most broken relationships can be salvaged!"* I am a firm believer in reconciliation. I have seen it take place in so many beautiful ways. But everyone must do their part. We live in a culture where more and more are going from one relationship to another, repeating a process that leaves broken hearts and battered dreams in their wake. Too many, when seeing a breakdown in a relationship, simply cut what they could not untie, like an old shoelace. No matter how much may have been invested in someone, it seems easier for some to junk the relationship and move on to the next. We do not do that with our automobiles. We make a major investment in a car, and if it doesn't start one

> Most broken relationships can be salvaged. But everyone must do their part.

morning, what do we do? Junk it? If we can't fix it, we call for help. We pinpoint the problem and get it fixed. If that is good sense for an auto repair, why isn't it good sense for relationships that have years of investment behind them? There are too many deposits of love and time invested in a relationship to just junk it when it sputters or has a flat tire.

When relationships are broken, our general tendency is to see ourselves only as the offended party. And this is exactly at the heart of why some of us live a lifetime with broken relationships discarded along our path of life. Few of us really want to admit that we are the offending party. It is usually someone else's fault in our minds. Few of us are keen on taking personal responsibility. We have been programmed since our childhood to point the finger of accusation at someone else. But isn't there a little of Onesimus in all of us? Could it be that as we continue reading his story, we have something to learn from him?

Onesimus went back! And he did so with sincere remorse and regret that led to genuine repentance. Philemon had no choice but to receive him and let the party begin. Perhaps you are Onesimus. It might be that, like him, you need to go back and admit a wrong when before you insisted that you were always right. Are you Philemon? Do you need to forgive someone who hurt or wronged you? Is there an experience from your own life in which you need to bury the hatchet? Paul has made plain the way. Let's read on.

16   THE OFFENDING PARTY

*A*s we've discussed, every broken relationship has an offending party. True reconciliation calls for a repentant heart on their part, a change of mind, a turn-around, a going back to someone with an admission of wrong and a request for forgiveness. Paul framed it like this to Philemon: "I am sending him [Onesimus]—who is my very heart—back to you" (Philemon v. 12 NIV).

Onesimus, the offending party, had become one "heart" with Paul. They were now more closely related as brothers in Christ through the blood of Jesus than to their own blood relatives who did not know Him. Since Christ had now transformed Onesimus's life, he had no option but to go back and make things right. The Greek word for this repentance literally means "to change one's mind." Onesimus had a genuine change of mind about his past actions. He was not headed home to argue his case. He was on his way back to admit his wrong and hopefully bury the hatchet with Philemon. Some of us make this journey back, but when we arrive on the scene, we try to justify our past actions or even argue our case. Not Onesimus. He was taking responsibility.

Let's revisit the story from chapter 1 about the Prodigal Son, the greatest short story ever told by Jesus. The prodigal was the offending party. He skipped out on his dad and left home with his inheritance. After wasting it all, he "came to himself" (Luke 15:17). He changed his mind about the entire ordeal. This led to a change of volition, of will, as he said, "I will arise and go to my father" (v. 18). And this resulted in a change of action when he got up and headed home. Repentance is a change of mind that affects a change of will that results in a change of action. And the father greeted the boy with open arms and a receptive heart that was void of retaliation or resentment. They buried the hatchet then and there. Onesimus, like the prodigal, was on his way home. He doesn't send a word of apology back from someone else. This was personal. He was going back himself.

When we have relationships that are based upon the solid foundation of being properly related to our source, the Lord Jesus, we are not out to escape our past, get a pass, or run from our mistakes. But a relationship with Him enables us to face our past, find a new beginning, and

make wiser choices going forward. Onesimus was headed home to Philemon to face the consequences of what he did and hopefully to make right his previous wrong.

This might be a different story today if Onesimus had sought counsel from some so-called professionals in the field today, instead of finding it in the wise counsel of the apostle Paul. Some today, after listening to his story, would have offered advice that said, "Look, forget about the past. You can find justification for what happened. Put it behind you. Go on with your life. Learn from your mistakes. Forget about Philemon." And had he taken counsel like this, he would have lived out his days, as many do today, with something left unfinished and a dark cloud that always hung over his head. That is no way to live a positive and purposeful life.

> A relationship with Jesus enables us to face our past, find a new beginning, and make wiser choices going forward.

Often the way forward is back. Back—to admit I was wrong in ways I always insisted I was right. Back—to make the previous wrong right. This is one of the great paradoxes of the Christian life. In God's economy, the way up is down, and the way down is up. Paul added an additional paradox to the equation that the way forward is back. He wrote, "I am sending him—who is my very heart—back to you" (Philemon v. 12 NIV). It was along these same lines of seeing that the way forward is back that Jesus said, "If you bring your gift to the altar, and there remember that your brother has something against you, leave your gift there before the altar, and go your way. First be reconciled to your brother, and then come and offer your gift" (Matthew 5:23–24). Do you see it? This is one of life's great paradoxes—the way forward is back!

This is the actual point of frustration with many of us, although it is seldom recognized as such. That is, we try to move on, to go forward, but something is left undone, and we must first go back in order to go forward. It just may be that unless someone reading these words goes back, forward progress will be thwarted, and future days will be spent in relational cul-de-sacs, roundabouts, or worse, dead ends. Only in Hollywood is such nonsense as "Love means never having to say you are sorry" successful. In real life, relationships do not succeed on that premise. Those who enjoy profitable, long-term relationships know what it is to go back to say, "I am sorry. I was wrong. Please forgive me."

> Only in Hollywood is such nonsense as "Love means never having to say you are sorry" successful. In real life, relationships do not succeed on that premise.

Onesimus gives us hope. If you think your particular case is hopeless, look at his. There is always hope for anyone who will admit to being the offending party. When we do, we can join Onesimus in some pretty good company. Moses, the highly revered emancipator of the Jewish people, was a murderer. But he discovered the way forward was back. After forty years on the back side of a desert, he went back and delivered a nation. And what about King David? He was exhibit A of an offending party. He stole the affections of another man's wife, got her pregnant, and even orchestrated her husband's demise and death. But later, plagued with remorse and repentance, he discovered the way forward was back. If anyone should doubt the sincerity of his repentance, simply read the Fifty-First Psalm. And let's not forget Jonah. He shook his fist in the face of God and His plan and later, while in the belly of a great fish, discovered the way forward was back. God gave him a second chance. Finally, no talk of the second chance would be complete without a mention of Simon Peter, the big fisherman. He did what he insisted he would never do. He denied he ever knew the Christ. But he, too, discovered the life-changing principle that the way forward is back. He went back, met Christ on the seashore in genuine repentance, and then did he ever go forward. Just read of his exploits in the book of Acts. When we go back, God forgives. And then we can move forward to our greatest days. The way forward is still back.

Who is it that gets the ball of reconciliation rolling? Both sides must do their part. There must be a repentant heart on the part of the offending party and a receptive heart on the part of the offended party. Relational difficulties persist when we who are the offending party become blind to our own abuses and refuse to admit we were wrong. After a while of continuing to try to justify our actions, we actually begin to believe the lie. Consequently, too many of us live out our days with unfinished business. The hatchet of broken relationships will never be buried until there is genuine repentance on the part of the offending party. The way forward is back!

17   THE OFFENDED PARTY

*E*very broken relationship has an offended party. Burying the hatchet calls for them to forgive when the offending party returns in genuine repentance. And it is imperative that this type of receptive heart be void of a spirit of retaliation or resentment. Philemon was the offended party in our story. The rift in the relationship did not occur because of anything he did. However, with Onesimus on his way home in genuine repentance, the ball of reconciliation was in Philemon's court. Would he welcome Onesimus back with pent-up resentment or, worse, with retaliation?

Many reconciliations never take place, and this is not always because the offending party is not truly remorseful, regretful, and repentant. It is because the offended party just can't bring themselves to forgive with a receptive heart. Hatchets cannot be buried until the offended party receives the one who has done them wrong with a truly forgiving heart.

Philemon had a golden opportunity for revenge and retaliation. In fact, by the Roman law of the day, Onesimus's crime could be punishable by death. Here was Philemon's opportunity for revenge and to teach a lesson for all who observed. At the very least, it was an opportunity for some good old-fashioned and self-inflicted resentment. After all, he had been wronged by a trusted confidant whom he had elevated in his service. In the end, reconciliation was now up to Philemon in the way he reacted to Onesimus's return.

In regard to receiving Onesimus back into good graces, Paul wrote to Philemon, saying, "Without your consent I wanted to do nothing, that your good deed might not be by compulsion, as it were, but voluntary" (v. 14). Paul could have pulled his apostolic rank and ordered the two men to reconcile for the sake of the gospel. But he was wise enough to realize that there could be no authentic reconciliation when it is forced, coerced, or manipulated. It must be voluntary. It must issue out of a willing heart, resulting in mutual consent.

Paul continued his letter to Philemon, "Perhaps he departed for a while for this purpose, that you might receive him forever" (v. 15). Yes, good can come from some of the most hurtful experiences. Paul said, "Perhaps." In essence,

he was saying, "Stop a moment. Think about it. Could it be there is a deeper reason?" He knew this was what God was saying to us through the prophet Isaiah: "'For My thoughts are not your thoughts, nor are your ways My ways,' says the LORD. 'For as the heavens are higher than the earth, so are My ways higher than your ways, and My thoughts than your thoughts'" (Isaiah 55:8–9). There was nothing presumptuous in Paul's use of the word *perhaps*. He was simply allowing room for something good to emerge out of what began as something bad.

> The beauty in the aftermath of mended relationships is that they can become productive learning experiences that ultimately result in our own good and God's own glory.

The beauty in the aftermath of mended relationships is that they can become productive learning experiences that ultimately result in our own good and God's own glory. Don't misunderstand what Paul was saying here. He was in no way condoning Onesimus's past actions. He was showing that we can triumph, even over our own wrongs and past mistakes.

Reading the words of verse 15—"Perhaps he departed for a while for this purpose, that you might receive him forever"—should remind us of Joseph and his own estrangement from his brothers. Most of us know the story found in Genesis 37–50 well. Joseph's brothers, filled with jealousy and resentment, sold him to a motley group of nomads on their way to Egypt. The brothers lied to their father, telling him they had found Joseph's coat of many colors soaked in blood and that he had no doubt been consumed by some wild animal. Meanwhile, down in Egypt, through a miraculous series of events, Joseph went from prison to the palace, rising in stature to become the prime minister of Egypt, the most progressive country on the planet in its day. And all of this happened by the time he was only thirty years of age. Famine came to Israel and brought these brothers to Egypt in hopes of finding grain. When finally confronted with their long-lost brother, they became filled with remorse and regret, and in the end, to make a long story short, a beautiful reconciliation took place.

The brothers were the offending party. Joseph was the offended party. The rift in the relationship had lasted for several years. The brothers were finally filled with repentance. But what would Joseph do? How would he respond to them after all those years of being wronged and living with the consequences of their own father thinking Joseph was dead for all those years? From the human standpoint, most of what had happened to Joseph was bad. Now he,

like all those who have been offended, found himself as the key to reconciliation. If he did not do his part, no matter how repentant his brothers were, it would be to no avail. But when he finally revealed himself to his brothers, he spoke these words: "Do not therefore be grieved or angry with yourselves because you sold me here; for God sent me before you to preserve life" (Genesis 45:5). God was in it all—and for a purpose. And then Joseph added, "You meant evil against me; but God meant it for good" (Genesis 50:20). Joseph saw the hand of God behind it all. How could he not receive his brothers with a receptive and open heart of forgiveness?

Yes, as Paul suggested, "Perhaps he departed for a while for this purpose, that you might receive him forever" (Philemon v. 15). It just might be that if you look deep enough, there is a "perhaps" written across your own experience.

18   AND IT CAME TO PASS

*O*ften when we are in the midst of relational challenges, it becomes hard to see anything good or worthwhile emanating from them. In Philemon 15, Paul considered the positive: "Perhaps he departed for a while for this purpose, that you might receive him forever." I love Paul's expression that Onesimus departed from Philemon "for a while." Difficulties are temporary. Broken relationships can be also. The most recurring phrase in the entire Bible is "and it came to pass." Most of our challenges in life have their own way of passing by after a while.

It is at this very point that we are reminded of what Paul wrote to his friends in Rome. Reminding them, and us, of an important truth, he wrote, "And we know that all things work together for good to those who love God, to those who are the called according to His purpose" (Romans 8:28). This truth is *confidential.* He began, "And we know." This truth is not understood by a world that has no relationship with Jesus Christ. It is a family secret

expressly for those in His family of faith. This truth is also *constructive.* Yes, "things work together for good." Not everything that happens is good. Onesimus's past actions, which resulted in a broken relationship, were not good. But God took even the bad things and after "a while" worked them together for everyone's good (Philemon v. 15).

It is also *comprehensive.* Look closely. Paul said "all" things are working together for good (Romans 8:28). I would never think to sit down and eat a bowl of flour or a tablespoon of baking soda. But when you put the two together and mix them up with a few other ingredients, I love the outcome—biscuits. All things, when woven together in the tapestry of the cross, work together for good after a while.

Finally, we should note that this truth is *conditional.* It is meant only for those who "love God . . . who are the called according to His purpose" (Romans 8:28). If we are the offending party in a broken relationship, our "purpose" is to repent with genuine remorse and regret. If we are the offended party, our "purpose" is to receive the repentant party back with a spirit that is void of revenge or resentment.

As Philemon read on, he came to these words calling on him to receive Onesimus back with open arms: "no

longer as a slave but more than a slave—a beloved brother, especially to me but how much more to you, both in the flesh and in the Lord" (Philemon v. 16). Do you see what can happen? There is often a deeper relationship *after* reconciliation than there ever was before the offense. The offended party does not soon forget the humility shown in the genuine repentance of the offending party. And the offending party does not soon forget the sweet release found in the forgiving and receptive heart of the offended party. No wonder Paul alluded to the fact that behind it all was a much deeper purpose that can result in a much deeper relationship. Yes, "perhaps he departed for a while for this purpose, that you might receive him forever" (v. 15).

> There is often a deeper relationship *after* reconciliation than there ever was before the offense.

Philemon's receiving Onesimus back "in the flesh" pointed to his reinstatement of his previous position (v. 16). Onesimus would work even harder because of his second chance. But that was not all. He was also returning as a beloved brother "in the Lord" (v. 16). This position is what lifts all our relationships to a higher and more mutually respected place as brothers and sisters, both connected to the Lord Jesus Christ through the new birth.

A new relationship in God's forever family does not free us from previous obligations and responsibilities. Paul was not suggesting this. He was seeking to open Philemon's eyes to a totally new type of relationship. On the socioeconomic level, things might well remain the same between the two men. But on the spiritual level, they became equals, brothers. Paul was stressing each individual's worth and dignity in the family of God, which leads to higher levels of respect in all our relationships.

Our interpersonal relationships are changed for the better when we are transformed from within by the love and power we find when we get plugged in to our source, the Lord Jesus Christ. We will never know what mended relationships can be on the highest level without identifying with Him. And this brings us back to the entire premise of the Connection Code: we will never properly relate to each other until we properly relate to ourselves, and we will never be able to exhibit a healthy sense of self-worth and self-esteem until we are properly related to our source of power and love, the Lord

> Our interpersonal relationships are changed for the better when we are transformed from within by the love and power we find when we get plugged in to our source, the Lord Jesus Christ.

Jesus Christ, through what is referred to as the new birth in John 3.

Leonardo da Vinci, the famous Italian artist perhaps best known for his depiction of *The Last Supper*, epitomized the value of mended relationships and buried hatchets. Though most of us are familiar with his famous painting of our Lord's last meal in the upper room, another story is told about him. It is said that while in the process of painting his masterpiece, da Vinci had a brutal and bitter altercation with a fellow painter. The master artist became so consumed and enraged over this that he plotted an evil scheme. When he painted the face of Judas along with the Twelve in the upper room, he painted the face of his adversary and thus portrayed him for all posterity as a traitor himself. As soon as da Vinci finished painting the face of Judas, everyone immediately recognized him as his present adversary. He continued his work, painting each of the disciples into the picture. Finally, it came time to paint the face of Christ. However, as much as he tried, one attempt following another, he could not bring himself to paint the Lord's face. Something strangely affected him. His own heart revealed to him that his hatred for his fellow artist was the heart of the problem. He found out that the

way forward was back—back to make amends, back to seek reconciliation, and back to repaint the face of Judas. Then with great liberty he painted the face of Christ, which believers have admired down through the ages.

Perhaps there is a "perhaps" in your own relationships. The way forward is back.

19   IT TAKES TWO

*R*econciliation is possible only when both the offending and the offended parties do their respective parts. It not only takes two to tango; it takes two to mend a broken relationship. The problem with many of us who find ourselves as the offended party in a relationship is not that we have a desire to retaliate, but that we harbor resentment. And this is often more detrimental to burying the hatchet with someone than anything else.

The most devastating effect of a spirit of resentment is not what it does to someone else but what it does to us. It can bring damage to us *physically*. Harboring resentment in our hearts is proven to have an adverse effect on such things as blood pressure and sleep quality. Some who find themselves eaten up with resentment over time find themselves eaten up with such physical challenges as ulcers or other damaging issues.

Resentment can also bring about a depressing effect upon us *mentally*. When allowed to consume us, it can

warp our capacity to think straight on matters of importance. Many people suffer from mental and emotional problems for the simple fact that they harbor deep resentment toward others and have lived for an extended period of time without forgiving past wrongs—even though the offending party has returned in genuine remorse and repentance, asking for forgiveness. Deep-seated resentment has its own way of damaging us physically and depressing us mentally.

But there is more. It also has a debilitating effect on us *spiritually.* It is not possible to have an effective prayer and Bible study life when harboring hatred or resentment toward someone else. Jesus warned, "When you stand praying, if you hold anything against anyone, forgive them, so that your Father in heaven may forgive you your sins" (Mark 11:25 NIV). One of the most damaging and dangerous issues with broken relationships is the effects they can have on the offended party when they simply cannot bring themselves to forgive. It damages us physically, depresses us mentally, and debilitates us spiritually.

> It is not possible to have an effective prayer and Bible study life when harboring hatred or resentment toward someone else.

Relationally speaking, the way forward is always

back—back to forgive and find a place of new beginnings. It was on this very point that Paul said, "Let all bitterness, wrath, anger, clamor, and evil speaking be put away from you, with all malice. And be kind to one another, tenderhearted, forgiving one another, even as God in Christ forgave you" (Ephesians 4:31–32). In our self-centered world, some people have a warped and wrong image of someone who forgives and begins again in a relationship. One who forgives is caricatured in the minds of some as one who is weak and wimpy. However, just the opposite is true. Forgiveness is not only a positive force but a powerful one as well. It takes someone with inner strength to forgive. Anyone can wallow around, harboring resentment with an unforgiving spirit. It takes no strength to do that. But it takes a person of strength and depth to be able to say and mean, "I forgive you. Let's start all over with a new slate and begin again."

> Forgiveness is not only a positive force but a powerful one as well. It takes someone with inner strength to forgive.

Think for just a moment about the individuals who have had the greatest impact on your own life. If you are like me, a few people will surface to mind, likely with a common characteristic. It wasn't simply that they surrounded

you with love, were always there for you, believed in you, or encouraged you. But each in their own ways forgave you of your faults. There were more times than I can remember when I disobeyed my dad. But he always forgave me and never brought it up again. As many times as I haven't measured up to being the husband I should be to Susie, she has always forgiven me and forgotten it. Forgiveness has a dynamic power in our lives. It helps bring out the best in all of us, regardless of whether we are on the giving or receiving end of the equation.

Reconciliation was set in motion with Philemon and his estranged friend, Onesimus, because both of them did their part to bury the hatchet. Onesimus returned with a genuinely repentant heart, and there is ample reason to believe Philemon received him back with a genuinely receptive heart. Often the pieces of broken relationships are never put back together because, as much as the offending party might deeply desire to see them mended, the offended party has become so consumed with resentment that they cannot bring themselves to truly forgive, much less begin again.

While Philemon and Onesimus have taken center stage in our relationship drama, someone else was playing a major part in their reconciliation. Look at Paul. He

stands in the middle, with Onesimus (the offending party) on one side and Philemon (the offended party) on the other. And he brought them together, one in repentance and the other with reception.

There is a much deeper truth here than the one with which we are dealing on the surface. In one sense, I am Onesimus. I am the offending party. The great Creator God made us to fellowship with Him. But we chose to go our own way, do our own thing, and leave Him out of our lives. For many years I had no personal relationship with Him whatsoever. The truth is, He is the offended party in my own drama. He provided a perfect paradise for all of us. But we thought we could do better. He wooed us and wooed us to Himself and ultimately gave the best that He could give, His only Son. Did we love Him? No, we nailed Him to a cross of execution. Jesus Christ, in a sense our Paul, came into the world to take us by one of His nail-scarred hands, reach up to the Father with His other, and bring us together in a relationship that will not simply last a lifetime but an eternity.

> Perhaps an Onesimus is reading these words. God is waiting and willing to receive you in forgiveness.

Perhaps an Onesimus is reading these words. God is waiting and willing to receive you in forgiveness. He

provides a new beginning, a land of beginning again. And the beautiful truth is, He has already buried the hatchet—deep into a Roman cross outside the city walls of Jerusalem almost two thousand years ago. There He demonstrated His love and His own receptive heart to any of us who would come home to him in repentance and faith.

I stood one cold winter day at that very spot outside the Damascus Gate in Jerusalem. We call it Skull Hill, Golgotha. The largest snowfall in decades had covered the landscape of the Holy City in a blanket of white. The snow was nestled into the crevices of the face of Calvary. The holes, which appeared like eye sockets, were filled with snow. The words of the ancient prophet Isaiah came quickly to mind: "'Come now, and let us reason together,' says the LORD, 'though your sins are like scarlet, they shall be as white as snow; though they are red like crimson, they shall be as wool'" (Isaiah 1:18). When we come home to Him in the spirit in which Onesimus returned to Philemon, God will receive us with open arms, no clenched fists, no crossed arms, just open arms of love and forgiveness. And then we can begin the great journey for which we were created in the first place, to know Him whom to know is life, abundant in the here and now and eternal in the then and there. It takes two! And He has already done His part.

20   TOTAL FORGIVENESS

*S*ome time ago on a trip to Amsterdam, my wife and I took a side trip to a little village called Haarlem. It was the scene of one of our life heroes, and her story had made an indelible mark on our young married lives years earlier. We departed the train and found our way to the cobblestone street called Barteljorisstraat. There on the corner still stands the little watch shop and above it the home of the Ten Booms.

Corrie ten Boom was the daughter of a Dutch watchmaker who hid Jews in their home during the days of the Nazi Holocaust. Eventually, as a young woman, she, along with her sister, Betsie, were arrested, interrogated, and sent to Ravensbruck, one of the infamous German concentration camps. There, Betsie died. Corrie survived and lived to tell her story in the bestselling book *The Hiding Place* and the motion picture by the same name. She related that years after the Nazi atrocities, she was invited to speak in a church in Munich nestled in the Bavarian Alps. There she saw a face she could never forget. Standing directly in front of her was the Nazi soldier who stood watch at the shower door in the processing center at Ravensbruck. She could never forget that face. Suddenly, the sights and sounds of that day all flashed back through her mind: the room filled with mocking, jeering men . . . the heaps of clothes piled in the corner of the room . . . and Betsie's scared, pained, and tormented face.

Now, years later, the soldier approached her with a radiant smile. "Fraulein," he began, "I am most grateful for your message. To think that, as you say, He has forgiven me of my sins." He offered his hand in reconciliation. Corrie ten Boom, who had spoken so often of the need to love and forgive, kept her hand back at her side. She recounted that she began to think to herself as vengeful as resentful thoughts flooded her mind: "I began to see the sin of my own thoughts. Jesus Christ had died for this man. Was I now going to ask for more? Lord Jesus, I prayed, forgive me and help me to forgive him."

Corrie tried to smile at the man. She couldn't. She struggled to extend her hand to him. She couldn't. She felt nothing. No love. No warmth. She then breathed a silent prayer, "Lord Jesus, I cannot forgive him. Give me Your forgiveness." As their hands clasped together an incredible thing happened. Into her heart leaped a love for this stranger that was over-powering.[4]

Corrie discovered that the world's healing hinges no more on our own forgiveness than it does on our own

> Along with the Lord's command to forgive others, He imparts the love we need to do so.

goodness. Along with the Lord's command to forgive others, He imparts the love we need to do so.

Remember, burying the hatchet takes two people doing two distinct parts. There must be a repentant heart on the part of the offending party. And there must be a receptive heart on the part of the offended party. Who are you as this drama plays out before us?

Are you Onesimus, the offending party? Be honest. Is there something you may have done in the past that brought about the breach in a relationship? Is there anything you may have left undone? You will never stand taller than when you go to that someone and voice those two liberating words, "I'm sorry." And accompany them with "I wronged you; please forgive me." Do it for your own sake. After all, the way forward is always back.

Are you Philemon, the offended party? Be willing to forgive. Let God help you forgive, and like Philemon and Corrie ten Boom and everyone else who walked this way,

you, too, will find it liberating. Harboring resentment hurts no one but you and can have damaging effects physically, mentally, and spiritually. Pass along the forgiveness you have found in Christ yourself to someone else in your life. It will set you free.

Perhaps you are neither Onesimus nor Philemon. Could it be that you are Paul? What the world needs is more men and women who help bring people together in reconciliation. If you know someone who is the offending party, care enough about them to help them see their need and then support them in the process. Perhaps you know someone who is the offended party; care enough to encourage them to forgive as Christ forgave them. You could be the key in helping to mend a broken relationship with a result in which everyone wins.

It may be that before you can forgive others for an offense, you need to forgive yourself and simply allow God to love you and fill you with His power and forgiveness. The place to begin is in your own confession to Him accompanied by a plea, "Please forgive me." He is willing and waiting, and you can begin the great adventure for which you were created in the first place: fellowship with Christ, a brand-new beginning with total forgiveness.

PART 5

CROSSING THE RUBICON
OF RELATIONSHIPS

If then you count me as a partner, receive him as you would me. But if he has wronged you or owes anything, put that on my account. I, Paul, am writing with my own hand. I will repay—not to mention to you that you owe me even your own self besides. Yes, brother, let me have joy from you in the Lord; refresh my heart in the Lord. Having confidence in your obedience, I write to you, knowing that you will do even more than I say.

—PHILEMON VV. 17–21

The year was 49 BC. The order came down to Julius Caesar to disband his army and give up his struggle. He stood on the banks of the Rubicon River and pondered his immediate dilemma. If he continued his march and crossed the river, there could be no turning back. He gathered his troops, tore up his orders, and led his dedicated legion across the Rubicon to march against Rome. This act of total commitment to the cause brought about a declaration of war against the Senate, and for Caesar, it paved the way to his becoming ruler of the expanding Roman world.[5] Since that moment, the phrase "crossing the Rubicon" has been used to signify total commitment to a cause from which there can be no turning back.

There should be a "Rubicon" in close interpersonal relationships, a line of commitment we cross in which we are "in" for the duration. The word *commitment* is one that gets a lot of wear today but needs a more definitive expression. Some are committed—but only to their own happiness. Thus, they tend to move from one relationship to another while being virtually void of commitment. Commitment is one of the missing elements in modern relationships. The secret to ongoing connections is to cross the Rubicon of relationships by making a commitment to one another that lasts a lifetime.

No treatise on the art of building positive and productive relationships would be complete without a word about commitment. Paul, having already addressed in his letter to Philemon such vital principles as affirmation of one another, accommodation of one another, and

acceptance of one another, next turned his attention to the importance of allegiance to one another. He expressed his commitment to Onesimus by writing, "If then you count me as a partner, receive him as you would me. But if he has wronged you or owes anything, put that on my account" (Philemon vv. 17–18). When Philemon read that, he knew Paul was unconditionally committed to Onesimus. Then Paul sent a definitive word to assure Philemon that he was just as committed to him as well by writing, "Having confidence in your obedience, I write to you, knowing that you will do even more than I say" (v. 21).

> Relationships that last over time are those that are built upon loyalty and commitment to one another.

Relationships that last over time are those that are built upon loyalty and commitment to one another. Crossing the Rubicon in relationships takes four steps. Paul articulately and accurately pointed each of them out as he continued his letter to Philemon. The first step is *openness*. And this is often the most difficult step, especially since any long journey always begins with the first step. Committed friends have no agendas hidden from each other. They are open in their relationships with each other.

The second step is *obligation*. Committed friends sense

a responsibility for one another. They always stick up for each other and rush to the other's defense when the need arises.

The third step in crossing this river is *objectivity*. They get the big picture. They return favors. They always see past themselves to the importance of reciprocation.

The final step is *optimism*. Committed friends believe the best about each other, stay positive, and always do more than is expected in their relationship. They bring out the best in each other. It only takes a little to be above average in this respect.

There is a river to cross in our relationships with one another. It may be that some of you stand on its bank, in a similar way that Julius Caesar did. It is time to commit—to the point you realize there will be no turning back. Every relationship has its own Rubicon. Let's begin the crossing with the first step.

21 STEP ONE: OPENNESS

*C*rossing the Rubicon of relationships begins with the first step: openness. Paul was open and honest with his friend Philemon. There was no hidden agenda. He wrote, "If then you count me as a partner, receive him as you would me" (Philemon v. 17). Loyal friends feel free to ask favors. They have a sense of openness, a freedom that exists in the relationship. They do not play games or try to subtly manipulate one another. They are open.

One of the signal characteristics of loyal friendships that endure over the decades is the element of transparency. Without an openness existing between each other, relationships never get beyond a superficial level. Honesty and openness are key ingredients to sustaining lasting relationships. We live in a culture where many people guard against opening up to anyone. There are a lot of paper faces on parade—that is, masks that some people wear in relationships and refuse to take off. This is what makes relationships a risky endeavor. The culprit in the

behavior is a fear of rejection. Some people put up a shield, constantly on guard against becoming vulnerable to anyone else. This built-in fear results in too many of us not taking the risk and stepping out in openness.

Paul was taking a giant step of openness with Philemon at this point in his letter. He took a risk, the risk of the possibility of being rejected. Not many take relational risks today. They spend their time calculating why others enjoy productive relationships and excusing why they cannot. Relationships are a risky business. Ironically, the very thing we sometimes seek to keep covered up when conversing with others is often the very thing, if we were open, that would attract others to us. For example, my own origins are rather humble, to say the least. For a time, I considered this detrimental to the development of some relationships. It sounds foolish now, but in my immaturity and insecurity, I sometimes sought to pretend to be someone I was not. When I became open with others about this very point, I found that what I thought was a deterrent was, in reality, an asset in the development of my own interpersonal relationships with others. We should not fear being open with others.

As we attempt to cross our own Rubicon in relationships, we will do one of two things with others: we will build a bridge, or we will build a barrier. When we build bridges instead of barriers, we will have more loyal and lasting friendships. What are you building? Are you erecting barriers so that no one can really look into your own heart? Do you, like I once did, fear rejection?

We all know what it is like to attempt to build a relationship with someone whose façade we could never seem to penetrate. They left us with the feeling that we were shut out of some of the deeper parts of their lives. They simply would not cross the Rubicon with us. They could not seem to take even this first step of openness. Many of us have found that in seeking to build relationships with others, some of those who seem to be the most secure and superior are, in reality, the least sure of themselves.

> Many of us have found that in seeking to build relationships with others, some of those who seem to be the most secure and superior are, in reality the least sure of themselves.

Are you building any bridges in your own relationships? This is not to suggest letting anyone and everyone cross over into the private turf of the hidden things of the heart. Openness with others is no call to reveal every single detail about our lives to anyone who will listen. We all have our private moments that are no one else's

business. We are talking about bridges here, not some wide-open autobahn or interstate highway. We are talking about the need to be open in our relationships with one another in the way Paul was with Philemon. Something wonderful happens when two people connect with each other in openness and honesty. Openness has its own way of building bridges in relationships.

This first step of openness is what made Jesus of Nazareth so winsome and warm in His own interpersonal relationships with others. He was transparent. He had no hidden agenda. He traveled daily with His friends. He ate with them. He prayed with them. He wept with them on occasion. He was a people person. He got involved in their personal struggles. He allowed people to look into His own heart and get to know Him. He told others of His own needs. And though it was risky, for some did reject Him, many others were drawn to this One who extended a bridge of openness to them.

Remember the woman at the well in Samaria? She had spent a lifetime building barriers until the day she met Him. Her past was marred with many haunting choices she sorely wished she could do over again. She had known so much rejection that she was scarred by a lack of self-worth and self-respect. But one day at a well, she met a

Man who told her everything she had ever done. And He built a bridge to her. She crossed over, opened up, and in so doing found a true friend for life.

As Paul opened himself to Philemon, he chose an interesting word in his letter that we translate as "partner." It is a word that describes one mutually shared life. Paul and Philemon were connected; they were united. Since Paul had already spoken of Onesimus as being his "own heart" (v. 12), Philemon knew that to reject Onesimus would be to reject Paul himself. Onesimus's journey back in repentance was hard enough in itself. But it could have been that much more difficult if met by those who didn't believe in second chances.

> We never have to be afraid of the truth. It always wins in the end, and as Jesus said in John 8:32, it is the one thing that can set us free.

Commitment is a key to lasting relationships. And the first step is openness. We never have to be afraid of the truth. It always wins in the end, and as Jesus said in John 8:32, it is the one thing that can set us free. Build a bridge of openness today with someone you know, and you will be on the way to crossing your own Rubicon.

22   STEP TWO: OBLIGATION

*T*he second step in getting across the Rubicon to the place of commitment in our relationships involves obligation. Paul sensed an obligation to his new and trusted friend Onesimus. He continued writing to Philemon, saying, "If he has wronged you or owes anything, put that on my account . . . I will repay" (Philemon vv. 18–19). Loyal and lasting friends always stick up for one another and have each other's backs. They live under obligation to each other. Through a strong sense of commitment, they are quick to rise to each other's defense in times of need.

Paul instructed Philemon to charge whatever Onesimus owed him to his own account. He was in no way suggesting that Philemon forget about Onesimus's past wrongs and ignore the debt. He sent Philemon this promissory note, written in his own hand, with its vow to pay. He was a committed friend. He was living out of an obligation that comes to each of us when we decide to cross the Rubicon in our commitment to someone else.

One of the obvious characteristics of genuine commitment in a relationship is this idea of mutual obligation. Many in our world today simply bounce from one relationship to another to another while always placing the blame for failure on the attitudes and actions of someone else. When it comes time to make a commitment in a relationship, it is easier for some people to just move on to another one rather than stepping out in openness accompanied by a sense of obligation. Relationships are a two-way street, and commitments involve not only openness but obligation as well.

> One of the obvious characteristics of genuine commitment in a relationship is this idea of mutual obligation.

Something beautiful was unfolding in the friendship of Paul and Onesimus. Paul was offering to pay a debt for which he was not personally responsible. Why? Because Onesimus owed a debt he could not pay. Paul assumed his debt and gave his word of promise to repay as well. In this very sentence of his letter, he was showing us his openness to Philemon and his obligation to Onesimus in the same breath.

Even though this sense of paying a debt we do not owe because a friend has a debt he or she cannot pay manifested

here in a horizontal relationship, it had its roots in a vertical relationship. There is a bit of Onesimus in each of us. We, like him, have gone our own way in rebellion against the One who loves us most and meets our needs. The Bible refers to what we owe as a sin debt. We cannot pay it. Just as Paul had nothing to do with Onesimus's sin and guilt, neither did Christ have anything to do with ours. And yet as Paul assumed this debt he did not owe, so the Lord Jesus made His way across His own Rubicon to a Roman cross to pay our debt. In essence, He was saying to His Father what Paul was saying to Philemon, "If he has wronged you or owes anything, put that on my account. . . . I will repay" (vv. 18–19). No wonder seven hundred years earlier Isaiah said, "All we like sheep have gone astray; we have turned, every one, to his own way; and the LORD has laid on Him the iniquity of us all" (Isaiah 53:6). We are talking real commitment here, accompanied by a sense of openness and obligation. Those of us who are in relationship with Jesus Christ can go to the computer in heaven, pull up our accounts, and beside our names are the words, *Paid in full.*

> Those of us who are in relationship with Jesus Christ can go to the computer in heaven, pull up our accounts, and beside our names are the words, *Paid in full.*

Feeling a sense of obligation to one another is the second step in finding true commitment in our relationships with others. Relationships endure through the years when those involved stick up for one another. I recall a time in years gone by when I was falsely accused, and a friend rose to my defense and passionately spoke up for me. Although today we are separated by hundreds of miles and decades of years, I will never forget his loyalty and the deeper bond that developed because of it. How much more do you imagine Onesimus became committed to Paul when he got wind of the fact that Paul had risen so strongly to his defense? And how much more would your own friends be committed to you if you proved beyond any doubt your unconditional defense of them?

Loyal and lasting friendships are built on a commitment that issues out of openness and obligation.

23 STEP THREE: OBJECTIVITY

*I*f openness and obligation are the first two steps to commitment in a relationship, then objectivity is the third. Look at Paul. He was objective in his relationships with others. In his letter to Philemon, he challenged him along the same lines, saying, "If he . . . owes anything, . . . I will repay—not to mention to you that you owe me even your own self besides. Yes, brother, let me have joy from you in the Lord; refresh my heart in the Lord" (Philemon vv. 18–20).

Loyal friends are objective. They get the big picture. They keep things in perspective. They can see past themselves to realize the importance of reciprocation. They are quick to return favors. *Commitment* is a lost word in many relationships today because so many of us are bent on getting what we can for ourselves, in place of a focus on giving. True and loyal friends bring out the best in each other because of their objectivity.

Recent generations have been characterized by a

prominent philosophy that advocates a mentality of "doing our own thing." Often this is accomplished through manipulation and self-assertion. For some, it is mostly about how to get leverage over the other person in a relationship. This has wreaked havoc on many interpersonal relationships. One of the major reasons for the trend of short-term relationships is a lack of objectivity. Some are overly focused on being on the receiving end of every relationship. Few seem to be objective enough to realize that reciprocity, the returning of favors, and giving of themselves are key for building lasting relationships.

> Few seem to be objective enough to realize that reciprocity, the returning of favors, and giving of themselves are key for building lasting relationships.

When our daughters were little, they loved going to the local neighborhood park. They especially loved to ride the seesaw. In my mind's eye, I can still see those two little toddlers now on it . . . up and down . . . up and down . . . up and down. Relationships can be like that . . . up and down. We might call it the seesaw effect. There are times in a relationship when one of the parties does most of the giving and the other does most of the receiving. Then circumstances change, the tables are turned, and the roles are

reversed. Anyone who has been married for any length of time knows of this law of reciprocation.

Imagine a wife whose husband has recently lost his job. Although he may not verbalize it, he is having a real struggle with his own self-confidence and self-worth. He becomes contentious and on edge. He says some things he really does not mean at all. He is not as affectionate and giving as he is normally. Money is dwindling. Fear is setting in. The wife is certainly not getting much from the relationship. The temptation for her is to pull away from him in frustration, to just give him space. Some might even run away under such conditions. But this wife is committed to the relationship. She is open, obligated, and objective. She realizes her husband needs to be on the receiving end of her unconditional love now more than ever, even though many would argue he does not deserve it. So she gives. And for a time, she gives far more than she receives.

Committed relationships get the big picture. They are objective. They can see past themselves and their own momentary needs to the importance of reciprocation. So they give. They understand that friends need friendship the most often when they deserve it the least.

This lack of objectivity is the point of breakdown

in many relationships. This need to always be on the receiving end, this inability to see the seesaw effect in every relationship, is a key factor in the destruction of many relationships. Get the big picture. Decide to be a giver. Return a favor. Hop on the seesaw. Make a lot of deposits in your relationships because there will come a time when you will need some withdrawals. Committed friends are objective and see the need to reciprocate with others.

> Make a lot of deposits in your relationships because there will come a time when you will need some withdrawals.

The words Paul wrote of a parenthetical nature in verse 19 are not lost in the discussion. When assuring Philemon he would be responsible for Onesimus's past debts, He slipped this word to Philemon: "not to mention to you that you owe me even your own self besides." We can only imagine what Philemon must have thought when he read this sentence. Be open, and don't forget to be objective.

24 STEP FOUR: OPTIMISM

*I*f there is one thing that can always be said about the apostle Paul, it is that he was optimistic. He saw an answer in every problem instead of a problem in every answer. He concluded this paragraph on the importance of commitment, saying, "Having confidence in your obedience, I write to you, knowing that you will do even more than I say" (Philemon v. 21). Paul was savvy enough to know that it is hard to feel good about someone else when we do not feel good about ourselves. He was letting Philemon know that he believed in him and that he was confident he would do the right thing. This optimistic approach on Paul's part yielded amazing results. It would bring out the best in Philemon. We bring out the best in others when we let them know we believe in them and are confident they will do even more than is asked or required. This spirit of optimism is a major step in achieving the fruition of commitment in our relationships. Committed friends believe in each other and come through for one another when the chips are down. In fact, as Paul revealed, they always do what is expected of them—and then some.

Can you imagine the emotions that must have been racing through Philemon as he continued to read this letter? Think about what he has read. Paul has dropped the Onesimus bomb, laid out the entire situation, and asked for a huge favor. He has in no uncertain terms shared his advocacy for Onesimus, and then he affirmed that Philemon would do more in the moment than he has even asked. He let Philemon know he believed he would do what was right—and all in advance of the fact. Just try to put yourself in Philemon's shoes.

Are you optimistic about matters in your own relationships? Do your friends and family know that they can rest in your confidence in them? Susie, my wife, and I have raised two daughters. Since their births there has not been a single day of their lives when they did not hear their father say, "I am proud to be your dad." In a thousand ways we sought to let them know we believed in them, we had confidence they would do the right thing when the need arose, and that we also believed they would do even more than we had asked of them. When you let others know that you believe in them, as Paul did with Philemon, it brings out the best in them far more quickly and with much more

> When you let others know that you believe in them, it brings out the best in them far more quickly and with much more lasting results than if you were to motivate them by fear.

lasting results than if you were to motivate them by fear, berating them over their perceived shortcomings.

Paul was not coercing Philemon. Neither was he commanding him to do something. Loyalty and commitment must come from one's own volition to be effective. Paul simply presented his case, expressed his confidence in both parties, and left the ball in Philemon's court. He knew that people have a way of becoming and doing what they are encouraged to be and do—not what they are manipulated or coerced into doing. Expecting the best out of others with an optimistic attitude and expressing confidence in them doing even more than is required of them goes a long way in motivating and moving them to do the right thing when the situation arises.

It is not difficult to drown out the fires of enthusiasm in others. Just pour on the cold water. Throw in your two cents' worth of negativity and discouragement. The world is filled with pessimists. But often a simple word of positive confidence in someone gives them the strength they need to move forward. Optimism brings out the best in all of us. When an athlete knows the coach believes in him, he gives the second effort. When an employee knows the boss believes in her, she works a bit harder. When a child has encouragement at home and knows her mom and dad believe in her, she climbs higher. Optimism is the giant step that helps us leap over the Rubicon in our own relationships.

What do you suppose Philemon did after reading this letter? I like to think he did what Paul requested and even passed on these positive principles to Onesimus. I think he let Onesimus know he now believed in him. The reason we can hold to this hope is in another letter that was penned in AD 115 and recently discovered. It is a letter from Ignatius, the church father from Antioch, written to the bishop of Ephesus. And the bishop's name? Onesimus. Our own Onesimus would have been in his seventies when the letter was received. It is entirely possible that Bishop Onesimus of Ephesus was indeed the same Onesimus who returned to Philemon. If so, his success in life was due, in large part, to the optimistic encouragement he found in his interpersonal relationships with his loyal brothers in the faith, Paul and Philemon. Their commitment to one another was built on openness. They were honest and open with one another. It was also built on obligation. They

sensed an obligation to be unconditionally committed to one another. Objectivity also played a significant part in the drama. They saw past their own individual needs and reciprocated with each other at the points of the other's needs. Finally, optimism won the day, as they believed the best of each other and challenged one another to excel.

There are four steps to loyal and committed relationships: Be open. Be obligated. Be objective. And above all, be optimistic.

25   STEP FIVE: OBSERVATION

$\mathcal{T}$he time has come to push the pause button and make some observations. Have you ever crossed the Rubicon with anyone? One who is open with you? One who senses his or her obligations in a relationship? One who rises to your defense when the need arises? Do you have a friend who is truly objective, one who understands the importance of reciprocation in a relationship and who gives as much as they take in the process? One who loves you even when you have been wrong and may least deserve it? Do you have a friend who is optimistic, one who always believes the best in you?

Perhaps a much more pertinent question is this: Are you a committed and loyal friend? Are you open with others in your inner circle? Or do you too often keep your guard up? Do you build barriers with others, or do you build bridges? Do you sense an obligation to anyone? Have you stood up for anyone recently? Are you objective? Or are you too quick to forget the investment others have made in your life? Are you slow to reciprocate? Do others see you as optimistic?

Building positive and productive relationships with others goes back to making sure we are firmly connected at the source through our own personal relationship with Jesus Christ—that is, getting plugged in to our spiritual power. Jesus has made a commitment to you. He crossed the Rubicon on a Roman cross to relate to you. He is open. He always builds bridges, never barriers. He defends you and will be your advocate before the Father in the coming day of judgment. He is objective, no respecter of persons. And in His optimism, He brings out the best in us.

> Jesus has made a commitment to you. He crossed the Rubicon on a Roman cross to relate to you.

Commitment seems to be a lost word in our modern vocabulary. There is a Rubicon in every personal relationship, a river we cross from which there is no turning back. Many get right up to the bank of the river, but that is as far as they get. But others go forward with four steps that lead to a moment of commitment. They know true commitment demands being open with one another, the ability to be honest and to take a risk. They also have a healthy sense of obligation to each other, always rising

to the other's defense. They are objective and optimistic, believing in each other and bringing out the very best in one another.

Most of us are fairly well versed in the art of commitment. We are committed to our jobs. We show up on time and put in an honest day's work. We are committed to all sorts of social clubs, athletic teams, garden clubs, and the like. We show up because we have made a commitment to the team. Many of us are quick to make up meetings of civic clubs if we miss them. We know a lot about commitment, and it is never more vital than in the art of building positive relationships.

In Paul's words, set out to refresh someone's heart this week. Do something for someone. Perform some act of kindness. Do someone a favor that is totally unsolicited. Pay someone a sincere compliment. Loyalty breeds loyalty in relationships.

If you need a few suggestions—refresh the heart of someone who regularly serves you at a local restaurant this week. Pay a compliment. Rise to his or her defense. Give an extra tip.

Refresh the heart of your husband or wife. Be objective about it. Give without expecting anything in return. Do a good deed that may even be out of character for you this

week. Buy her some flowers. Write a letter, and stick it in his briefcase.

Refresh the hearts of your children. Some of us are committed to a lot of things but not to fatherhood. Cross the Rubicon with your kids. Let them know how much you believe in them to do the right thing. With an optimistic spirit, let them know you are proud of them and you will help bring out the very best in them.

Refresh the heart of a friend. Take a risk. Be open. Let someone have a peek into your own heart. Build a bridge. Honesty and openness will get you started. Believe in someone—and let them know it.

There should be a "Rubicon" in every close inter-personal relationship, a line of commitment we cross in which we are "in" for the duration. Commitment is one of the missing elements in modern relationships. The secret to ongoing connections is to cross the Rubicon of relationships by making a commitment to one another that lasts a lifetime.

PART 6

ACCOUNTABILITY: DON'T
LEAVE HOME WITHOUT IT

*But, meanwhile, also prepare a guest room for me, for I
trust that through your prayers I shall be granted to you.
Epaphras, my fellow prisoner in Christ Jesus, greets you,
as do Mark, Aristarchus, Demas, Luke, my fellow laborers.
The grace of our Lord Jesus Christ be with your spirit.
Amen.*

—PHILEMON VV. 22–25

*O*ne of the reasons my family buys our cars from
a particular local dealership is because of their
dedicated service department and their determined servant spirit. Periodically, I take my car in for a complete
checkup. The service manager makes certain my automobile is properly maintained so that as the miles add up, it

will continue to run smoothly with minimal mechanical maladies.

Like many of you, my wife and I are fortunate enough to own our own home. Or, to be more accurate, the mortgage holder actually owns it. Periodically, we give it a checkup. Recently we made some repairs on the eaves of the roof. It wasn't leaking—yet. Some wood had begun to rot around one of the eaves, and it was only a matter of time before bigger problems would come. So, we did some preventive maintenance.

I have a body. Some might argue that at my advancing age, it is not much of one. But it is still a body nonetheless. Every year I go to my physician for an annual physical. It is quite extensive and takes up most of the day. We make certain everything is in proper working order and seek to detect any abnormalities or possible problems developing. Along with my annual exam, I try to watch my diet and exercise regularly. It is called preventative medicine, and I am a big believer in seeking to practice it.

Much of what goes wrong with my automobile, my house, or my body for that matter does so because of one word: *neglect*. No checkup. No maintenance. No accountability. *Accountability*—now that is an important word. If it is good for cars and homes and bodies, why is it a forgotten discipline in our personal relationships? It is good for husbands and wives from time to time to push the pause button, sit down, focus, and check up on their relationship with one another. It is good for parents to do the same with their children and for friends to stop long enough to perform some preventative maintenance on long-standing relationships.

> It is good for husbands and wives from time to time to push the pause button, sit down, focus, and check up on their relationship with one another.

As Paul concluded his letter to Philemon, he wanted him to know that he was going to hold him accountable and visit to check on his ongoing relationship with Onesimus. He wrote, "Also prepare a guest room for me, for I trust that through your prayers I shall be granted to you" (Philemon v. 22). That sentence could mean only one thing, and Philemon knew well what it meant. Paul was going to stop in at a later date to check up on the relationship. He was sending a message that he intended to hold Philemon accountable. Paul was wise. He knew that what went wrong in many relationships did so because of neglect. No accountability. No checkups. No maintenance in relationships.

Accountability is a big part of success in life. We all need

it, and more than most of us ever realize. We need accountability in our marriage relationships. Marriages that last are those that practice preventive maintenance and hold each other accountable. When accountability goes, damaged relationships follow quickly. I am accountable to my wife. I do not just go my own way, telling her that what I do and when I do it is none of her business. It *is* her business. We are one. We have a unique relationship because we are accountable to one another for what we do, where we go, and how we behave.

We all know something of accountability. We practice it every day in many various venues of life. We have it at the office. We do not just show up to work on Monday morning whenever we desire or decide not to show up at all. We arrive at an appointed time and work a certain number of hours if we expect to be remunerated for our service. Some of us in sales are accountable for quotas, producing a certain amount of sales and new business. Profitable businesses are successful in large part because of a process of accountability that permeates the workplace.

And what about national, state, and local governments? As citizens we need laws to govern our behavior and to protect us. We need to be held accountable when we drive through stop signs or exceed the speed limits. A lack of accountability from governments would result in a state of total anarchy. Accountability is a part of our everyday life. In one way or another, we are faced with it at every turn of the corner.

We have accountability in our schools. Teachers should hold students accountable for their studies and homework. They should administer scheduled testing procedures to ensure accountability. No one should graduate with an earned degree without being held accountable for the required assignments. So much of every aspect of our lives is filled with the knowledge that we need accountability to succeed.

And what about the athletic arena? We see accountability playing a huge role there also. If an athlete refuses to attend scheduled practice sessions, he will not see playing time when the real games begin. In high school and college basketball, if a player commits five fouls in a single game, he is disqualified from the game by the referee. All athletes are accountable to their coaches, teammates, officials, umpires, and referees on the playing field.

It is strange that, although we daily practice accountability in virtually every area of life, when it comes to personal relationships with friends, most of us seem to see no need for it.

Accountability measures surround us every single day. Many of us have mortgages on our homes that come with regularly scheduled monthly payments. We are held accountable to pay these on time or certain penalties will arise. If we go months without payments, we are in danger of the lender foreclosing on our property.

What do these things tell us? Accountability plays a significant part in all we do in life. It is strange that, although we daily practice accountability in virtually every area of life, when it comes to personal relationships with friends, most of us seem to see no need for it.

It is little wonder we have an epidemic in our world of short-term relationships that never evolve into long-term ones. If accountability is imperative for government, education, athletics, health, and business dealings, it is also an imperative incentive for developing lasting positive and productive relationships that stand the test of time.

When I was a new believer still in my teen years, I met and made a best friend whose friendship has lasted across the decades. Jack Graham and I began to take note of what was happening around us. We watched some of our classmates literally destroy their young lives through alcohol, drugs, and illicit sex. Although as teenagers we did not know what to call it, we entered into an accountability

relationship with one another, determined to help each other. We made a promise to God and to each other to keep ourselves pure and clean. We held one another accountable, and to this day, more than five decades later, he remains a friend who "sticks closer than a brother" (Proverbs 18:24) and to whom I remain accountable.

As we each look back over our lives, we can attest to seeing many destroyed relationships in the lives of others, and perhaps a few in our own were left stranded along the way. What destroys our relationships? The answer can be found in attitudes of self-reliance, self-righteousness, self-sufficiency, and self-centeredness. *Accountability* has become the lost word in many relationships, with devastating results. The lack of it has been the downfall of so much potential and promise. Accountability is the "ability" to be open and allow a small number of trusted, loyal, and committed friends to speak truth into us in love. We should only be accountable to those who have our best interests always in mind. We all need a person from whom we can receive wise counsel and willing correction.

Perhaps there is no other word as

> What destroys our relationships? The answer can be found in attitudes of self-reliance, self-righteousness, self-sufficiency, and self-centeredness.

feared by some as that word *accountability*. It is against our very nature to want to be held accountable for anything, especially related to our own actions or attitudes. Some of us fear it because we mistake it for something else. Some of us may think it means only put-downs, criticisms, or rebukes from those who seem to take delight in seating themselves in some kind of chair of judgment of others. Remember, we are talking about accountability from a very select, limited number of true friends who always have our best interests at heart—much like the relationship of Paul and Philemon. Relationships are doomed to defeat without the element of accountability. We all need it.

Paul was signaling in this section of his letter that accountability in our relationships calls for three important views. First, *insight*. Paul concluded this letter by letting Philemon know he was coming by to check up on how things were going with his relationship with Onesimus. *Hindsight* also plays a role in effective accountability. It involves an investment of time and interest. We need to have the hindsight to see that every arena of our relationships (affirmation, forgiveness, acceptance, and commitment to one another) that Paul had previously addressed is of vital importance. Finally, Paul was signaling here that *foresight* is imperative. Paul concluded

his letter with the prayer that grace might rest upon his trusted friend. We need the foresight to see that we all need a little more grace to make our relationships what God intends them to be. Accountability. We all need it. Don't leave home today without it.

26 ACCOUNTABILITY INVOLVES INSIGHT

*W*e have now arrived at the finale of Paul's epistle to Philemon—and to us: "But, meanwhile, also prepare a guest room for me, for I trust that through your prayers I shall be granted to you" (Philemon v. 22). In my mind's eye, I can see Philemon, perhaps with his chin cupped in his hand, as he read, *Oh yes, and one more thing, get the guest room ready for me; I am coming to visit.* Paul was being a bit subtle, but the message was loud and clear, as if he were warning, "I am stopping by for the express purpose of seeing how the relationship is going between you and Onesimus, and whether you have followed through with my concerns in this letter." In this verse, spelled in big, bold capital letters, was the word *ACCOUNTABILITY*!

There can be little doubt that Philemon had the insight to see that the prospect of Paul's visit was a motivating factor in making sure his relationship was made right with the remorseful and repentant Onesimus. We all need accountability. It serves to help us do the right thing, what we ought to do in our relationships. When we speak of holding each other accountable, this does not mean making threats. Some confuse this issue. Paul was not indicating that unless Philemon did the right thing, he would have little to do with him in the future. Those whose accountability measures are based on threats will have tenuous relationships that are subject to performance. Not Paul. He built his relationships on such things as affirmation, affection, acceptance, and accountability. And he challenged us to go and do likewise.

> Those whose accountability measures are based on threats will have tenuous relationships that are subject to performance.

There is a subtle insight in this letter that can only be revealed when it is read in the original language in which Paul penned it, Koine Greek. When he stated that he hoped "through *your* prayers I shall be granted to *you*" (v. 22, emphasis added), both the *you* and *your* are in the plural number. This is not only subtle but significant. Paul was reminding Philemon that others were watching. Thus, we discover the insight that accountability calls for us to become transparent, touchable, teachable, and truthful.

Accountability calls us to be transparent with our

friends. Everyone needs someone with whom they can be genuinely open, honest, and candid. This vulnerability carries with it the risk of being wounded. But transparency is imperative if we are ever to be truly accountable to one another.

Those who live in accountability relationships must also be touchable. That is, we must be accessible and approachable, especially to those with whom we entrust our transparency. To his friends in Rome, Paul wrote, "I myself am confident concerning you . . . that you also are full of goodness . . . able also to admonish one another" (Romans 15:14). Earlier he stated in a letter to his friends in the region of Galatia, "Let us not become conceited, provoking one another, envying one another" (Galatians 5:26). To be in an accountability relationship demands transparency but also that we are touchable, accessible, approachable, and open with pure motives.

Relationships profiting from genuine accountability also have the element of teachability. We should never stop learning. It is a dangerous time in a relationship when one of the parties begins to feel as if he or she has all the right answers and no longer possesses a teachable spirit. This insight requires a spirit of humility. We should never get to the point at which we feel we can no longer learn from

one another or teach one another, for that matter. King Solomon said it best: "As iron sharpens iron, so a man sharpens the countenance of his friend" (Proverbs 27:17).

Those accountable to one another must also be truthful. Many of us cannot be held accountable because of a spirit of deception. We become so deceived in our thinking processes that we are totally convinced that any issue that arises in relationships is always the fault of someone else. Some of us have left dozens of relationships in our wake across the years, and in our own minds, we are convinced that we were not responsible for the breakup of a single one of them. We are deceived. Without total truthfulness in relationships, there can never be accountability.

Certain people among us live in a perpetual state of denial. Then others of us live daily in defeat. We all need someone with whom we can be honest and truthful to the core. It is extremely therapeutic to have a faithful friend in whom we trust and with whom we can be truthful, even when the truth hurts. We never have to be afraid of the truth. It always wins in the end, and Jesus said this is the very attribute that has a liberating effect on us: "You shall know the truth, and the truth shall make you free" (John 8:32).

For example, take the well-known case of King David

and Bathsheba. Like so many today, he tried his dead level best to cover up his sin. He did not want any of his family or friends to know about it. But he was fortunate to have a true and trusted friend, Nathan, who held him accountable. Nathan cared enough to confront David when he saw he was on a collision course. And when he did so in confidence and love, David came clean. It hurt. But it also eventually healed. Nathan kept his friend from greater hurt and heartache. It worked because their relationship with one another was transparent, touchable, teachable, and truthful.

Too many of us have had personal friends we observed heading in the wrong direction on a road that led to a dead end. But we let them go. Some of us simply do not care enough to confront others with compassion. Real friends are those who hold real friends accountable.

> Real friends are those who hold real friends accountable.

The subject of accountability comes with a warning. Being accountable does not suggest open season. Paul was not advocating for us to open up our lives to anyone and everyone. And in particular, this does not mean becoming accountable to those who have the decidedly unspiritual gifts of gossip and judgment and who perform them with frequency. Stay away from those types of folks. They do not have your best interests at heart. They usually end up hurting you instead of helping you. Paul was talking about accountability with a very small number of loyal, affirmative, forgiving, and committed friends who have earned the right to ask the hard questions. It was wise Solomon who admitted, "Faithful are the wounds of a friend" (Proverbs 27:6).

Accountability calls for insight on our part. Paul lets Philemon know in advance that he was coming by for the express purpose of checking up on him. We all need a Paul, someone who provides a measure of accountability in our relationship. Knowing there is a day when we will need to give account of our actions to someone motivates us to be more conscientious about our task. Accountability calls for insight, the discernment that shows us how much we need to be transparent, touchable, teachable, and truthful.

27 ACCOUNTABILITY INVOLVES HINDSIGHT

*A*ccountability becomes possible when we have the hindsight to see we have made an investment of time and interest in someone's life that earned us the right to hold them accountable, as well as to be held accountable ourselves. Paul concluded his letter by sending Philemon greetings from five mutual friends in the faith, a subtle reminder to Philemon of those men with whom they both had mutually beneficial relationships in the past: "Epaphras, my fellow prisoner in Christ Jesus, greets you, as do Mark, Aristarchus, Demas, Luke, my fellow laborers" (Philemon vv. 23–24).

These five mentioned men were not named at random, but in hindsight Paul laid out their names for a definite purpose. He was a master at the art of connecting people with each other. Throughout the letter Paul has dealt with five major contributing factors to productive relationships: affirmation, accommodation, acceptance, allegiance, and

accountability. In hindsight, each of these five men mentioned was included to illustrate how these five contributing factors play out in our interpersonal relationships.

Paul began his letter to Philemon with a paragraph on the importance of affirmation, a genuine pat on the back. It was no coincidence he listed the name of Aristarchus among these five individuals. Aristarchus was Paul's traveling companion on his third missionary journey throughout the Mediterranean world and was arrested by the authorities in Ephesus. He had been through thick and thin with Paul while traveling with him. Aristarchus went all the way to Rome with him, encouraging and affirming him along the way. Paul revealed that they had a synergy together that was strengthened by their mutual affirmation of one another.

Paul also mentioned a man named Luke. He was Dr. Luke, by the way. In his letter to the Colossians, the apostle referred to Luke as his dear friend and doctor, "the beloved physician" (Colossians 4:14). Paul mentioned Luke here so that, in hindsight, Philemon would be reminded of how important it was to be in win-win relationships, accommodating one another.

Luke was a gentile. In that ancient day, most Jews, like Paul, would have no dealings with him. But Paul and Luke

had something to offer each other, and both benefited from their mutual friendship. Luke accompanied Paul on his second missionary journey and tended to his physical needs, which were many. There is little doubt that Luke's medical skills ministered to Paul on many occasions after stoning and beatings and likely added years to his life. Luke had watched on more than one occasion when Paul was stoned and beaten so severely that he was left for dead.

Paul also had a physical malady that he saw as a "thorn in the flesh" (2 Corinthians 12:7) that may have been his poor and failing eyesight. Luke was there beside him. They needed each other and lived in what we would call a win-win relationship. Philemon knew about all this, and the moment he read Luke's name in the letter, he must have thought about Paul's words a few paragraphs earlier about Onesimus now being "profitable to you and to me" (v. 11).

Paul also made much of calling on Philemon to receive Onesimus back in total forgiveness. Thus, he mentioned a man named Mark. Philemon's mind would race back in hindsight to remember that Mark stood as a testimony of Paul's own ability to forgive. It was young Mark who accompanied Paul on his first missionary journey as they departed from the church at Antioch. But Mark quit along the way. He went AWOL when the going got tough. Twelve

years had since passed, and this was the first mention of Mark in any of Paul's writings. Obviously they had buried the hatchet, and Paul had extended his forgiveness to him. And just in case there might be a lingering doubt in anyone's mind whether their new relationship was flourishing, Paul mentioned him in his last recorded letter to Timothy, written from prison in Rome shortly before his own execution. He said, "Only Luke is with me. Get Mark and bring him with you, for he is useful to me for ministry" (2 Timothy 4:11). Mark knew what it meant to be forgiven and, thus, to be accountable.

Paul's forgiveness and insistence upon accountability paid off in the end. Mark went on to write the second Gospel. As Philemon continued to read this letter, the mention of Mark's name must have spoken volumes to him about the necessity of forgiveness. Then, in hindsight, he had no option but to restore his broken relationship with his former friend who, like the Prodigal Son, was already on his way home in repentance.

Paul mentioned a man by the name of Epaphras. It should have been no surprise to Philemon that Paul did so to illustrate the importance of commitment in relationships. This man's life was characterized by total commitment to his friends. In the Colossians letter, Paul

said, "Epaphras, who is one of you, a bondservant of Christ, greets you, always laboring fervently for you in prayers, that you may stand perfect and complete in all the will of God. For I bear him witness that he has a great zeal for you" (4:12–13). This man so crossed his own Rubicon of relationship with Paul that he journeyed to Rome and volunteered to share Paul's imprisonment with him there. He was a well-known friend of Philemon, coming from the same hometown. His very name was synonymous with commitment, and Paul knew when Philemon saw it there, it would be a reminder of how important commitment is in our close relationships.

Finally, Paul mentioned the name of Demas to illustrate that accountability plays a prominent role in a long-term and productive interpersonal relationship. Demas's own story ends on a lamentable note. Paul mentioned to Timothy that "Demas has forsaken me, having loved this present world, and has departed for Thessalonica" (2 Timothy 4:10). Demas was a sad commentary to the fact that without accountability, long-term relationships have little hope of survival. By mentioning these five mutual friends, each illustrative of a paragraph in his letter to Philemon, Paul was reminding us all that we need each other. We need to be connected to our source,

the Lord Jesus, but we also need to be connected to each other, drawing from one another's support and strength.

In hindsight, we see that this principle of accountability was what Paul effectively and continually used to develop his own productive and mutually beneficial relationships. It often takes hindsight to see that accountability is based on loyalty to one another. We would not want to make ourselves accountable to anyone who did not have our best interests at heart. Paul kept around him a small group who were committed to one another and bent on affirming one another. This is not simply what the world needs now; it is what you and I need now. To grasp the importance of accountability, we need insight and hindsight. But we also need foresight.

> We need to be connected to our source, the Lord Jesus, but we also need to be connected to each other, drawing from one another's support and strength.

28 ACCOUNTABILITY INVOLVES FORESIGHT

*P*aul concluded this letter with a benediction that flowed from his poignant pen: "The grace of our Lord Jesus Christ be with your spirit" (Philemon v. 25). In so doing, he was indicating the necessity of having the foresight to know that we need grace and that without it, there is little hope of authentic accountability in our relationships. Many of us have a warped idea of what really constitutes accountability. We too often equate it with judgment, while Paul equated it with grace. Accountability is not about judging one another's faults; it issues from God's mercy and grace and results in a mutual love and respect among friends.

Grace is lacking in many relationships. *Grace* can be defined as unmerited favor extended toward someone. While mercy is not getting what we deserve, grace is getting what we do not deserve. And if grace is good enough for us to receive it from God, it is also good enough to extend to others in our relationships. Grace is the key that unlocks the door to accountability. We all need the foresight to see that extending grace to others is essential for building healthy relationships. If you make a mistake with someone in one of your relationships, make sure you err on the side of mercy and grace and not on the side of judgment.

> If you make a mistake with someone in one of your relationships, make sure you err on the side of mercy and grace and not on the side of judgment.

Paul was letting Philemon know that what he was calling him to do—receive Onesimus back in total forgiveness—was going to take an extra portion of God's grace to accomplish. It is not naturally in us to forgive and reconcile. Onesimus was already headed home. Philemon now knew he had no choice but to receive him and forgive him, and he was reminded it would take grace to do so. God's grace, His unmerited favor, is what we all need in our relationships. Grace is what empowers us to go forward with the foresight to see we cannot offer it out of our own strength. Until we know what it is to receive the grace of God in our own vertical relationship with Him, it is impossible to extend it to others in our horizontal relationships with them.

Paul prayed that the grace of God be with Philemon's "spirit" (v. 25). This was by design, not simply a phrase tacked on to the end of the letter. The spirit of man is that part of us that differentiates us from the rest of the created order. It is that part of us that connects with the Lord Himself. We need this foresight to see that if we are not in a proper relationship with the Lord, it will be virtually impossible to properly relate to others. We need grace. We need to extend it in our family relationships. We need it in the marketplace as we relate to others during the week. We are all in need of getting what we may not necessarily deserve. Accountability cannot exist without a measure of grace.

With this important reminder about grace, Paul closed this intensely personal and intimate letter to Philemon about our relationships. Although removed now by two millennia, it is a powerful word for us today. It is as up-to-date and relevant as the latest bestselling book on relationships in the marketplace. It calls to mind the importance of regularly giving one another a genuine pat on the back, a word of encouragement. It brings us into win-win relationships, which become mutually beneficial and not just one-sided. It speaks to us of the need to bury the hatchet by extending forgiveness to those who come to us in remorse and repentance. It calls upon us to cross our own Rubicon by making a new commitment to our own relationships with others. And it concludes with the importance of accountability to each other. We need each other.

If a periodic maintenance checkup is important to the performance of my automobile, my home, and my own physical well-being, it is good for my interpersonal relationships as well. Much of what goes wrong with these material elements of my life does so because of one word: *neglect*. No accountability. No checkup. No maintenance. The knowledge that someone near and dear to me is going to hold me accountable motivates me to have the foresight to do the right thing. Paul let Philemon know he was coming by to check up on him. The anticipation of such a visit from someone he loved and respected would spur him on to obey the wishes found in this personal letter from his trusted friend.

We have come now to the end of the letter—and to the end of another volume in the Code Series of devotionals. What do you suppose happened? Did Philemon do what Paul asked? Did he receive Onesimus back with open arms as a "beloved brother" (v. 16)? Did he forgive him? Did he restore him? The answer to these questions remains

shrouded in silence. We don't really know. But these are not the most important or pertinent questions. The question is not "What did Philemon do?" The real question is "What will you do now with the Onesimus who is in your life?" Perhaps the issue has been left unanswered so that you can complete the story in your own experience. And it will take grace to do so.

Thus, we conclude as we began back in the beginning of this book. We will never properly relate to each other until we possess a positive self-worth. And this will never happen until we discover our position in Christ and Christ's position in us by becoming properly related to Him and the grace He extends to us. This has always been, and will always be, the bottom line in all our relationships.

Let's close with some practical pointers:

1. We need accountability in our outward relationships with others. Build a bridge to someone this week. Stop building barriers. Give a pat on the back to someone who could really use it. Forgive a friend. Stop harboring resentment. Learn to say "I am sorry," or better yet, "Please forgive me." Then move forward. Cross your own Rubicon in a relationship with someone you treasure so that

there is no turning back from it. Be vulnerable yourself. We all need an accountability partner—someone we can trust. Extend grace.

2. We need accountability with ourselves in the inward expression of relationships. Take an honest self-assessment and inventory of your past relationships. Could there be the slightest possibility that you hold some of the blame for a failed relationship? Take personal responsibility. Hold yourself accountable. List some things you might have done differently if you had to do it all over again. Then put those things into practice with someone this week. And by the way, forgiveness should not be extended only to the other party. There are times when you should extend it to yourself. Forgive yourself and move on.

3. Ultimately, we all need to be accountable to God, our upward relationship. There is a day already fixed on God's calendar when "each of us will give an account of ourselves to God" (Romans 14:12 NIV). In anticipation of that coming day, have the foresight to see that even though you may neglect the need for accountability with others, or even yourself, you will ultimately be accountable to the

One who loves you most and gave Himself for you. Get properly connected to Him through faith in the Lord Jesus, and you will awaken to a brand-new you. Positive and productive relationships will then be the natural outcome of a life that is connected at the source of all things, the Lord Jesus Christ.

EPILOGUE

*I*t may be that, while you have been journeying through these pages, God's Spirit has been nudging you to believe His promises and to put your faith and trust in Christ for the forgiveness of your sin and receive God's free promise of eternal life. After all, heaven is God's personal and free gift to you. It cannot be earned, and neither is it ever deserved. We are all sinners, and each and every one of us have fallen short of God's perfect standard for our lives. Yes, God is a God of love, but He is also a God of justice and, therefore, must punish sin. This is where Jesus stepped in. He is the holy and sinless God-man who came to take your own sins upon Himself and die on the cross in your place as punishment for those sins. But just knowing this fact is not enough. You must transfer your trust from your own human effort to Christ alone, placing your faith in Him, and in Him alone.

If you would like to receive this free gift of eternal

life right now, it is yours for the asking. One of the most pointed and precious promises in all the Bible is found in Romans 10:13: "Whoever calls on the name of the Lord shall be saved." Believe it, and you can join Simon Peter in his prayer on the Sea of Galilee. Say it: "Lord, save me!" (Matthew 14:30). The following is a suggested prayer you can pray right now, from your own heart, no matter where you are.

Dear Lord Jesus,
I know I have sinned. I know that, in and of myself, I do not deserve eternal life. Please forgive me for my sin. Thank You for taking my sin upon Your own body and dying on the cross on my behalf and in my place. I believe Your promise that by calling on You I can be saved. I trust in You as the only One who can save me from an eternity of being separated from a holy God. Come into my life. Lord, save me. I accept Your free and gracious offer of forgiveness, abundant life, and eternal life with You. Thank You, Lord, for coming into my life this very moment as my very own personal Lord and Savior.

A simple prayer cannot save you. But Jesus can—and

will. After all, He promised! If this prayer has expressed the desire of your heart, you can now claim another of the promises Jesus made to those who believe in Him: "Most assuredly, . . . he who believes in Me has everlasting life" (John 6:47).

You can now join millions of Christ's followers who stand upon and believe His scriptural promise from John: "These things I have written to you who believe in the name of the Son of God, that you may know that you have eternal life, and that you may continue to believe in the name of the Son of God" (1 John 5:13).

Now, don't keep these promises all to yourself. What good is good news if you don't share it? Tell someone of your newfound faith in Him.

MISSION:DIGNITY

*A*ll the author's royalties and any additional proceeds from the Code Series (including *The Connection Code*) go to the support of Mission:Dignity, a ministry that enables thousands of retired ministers (and, in most cases, their widows) who are living near the poverty level to live out their days with dignity and security. Many of them spent their ministries in small churches that were unable to provide adequately for their retirement. They also lived in church-owned parsonages and had to vacate them upon their vocational retirement. Mission:Dignity tangibly shows these good and godly servants they are not forgotten and will be cared for in their declining years.

All the expenses for this ministry are paid out of an endowment that has already been raised. Consequently, anyone who gives to Mission:Dignity can be assured that every cent of their gift goes straight to one of these precious saints in need.

Find out more by visiting www.missiondignity.org or call toll-free 877-888-9409.

NOTES

1. Dale Carnegie, *How to Win Friends and Influence People* (New York, Simon & Schuster, 1936), 23.

2. Matt Bonesteel, "Gale Sayers's Speech in 'Brian's Song' Is an Essential Piece of Sports-Movie History," *Washington Post*, September 23, 2020, https://www.washingtonpost.com/sports/2020/09/23/gale-sayers-death/.

3. Ann O'Neill, "The Reinvention of Ted Turner," CNN.com, November 17, 2013, https://www.cnn.com/2013/11/17/us/ted-turner-profile/index.html.

4. Corrie ten Boom, "Corrie ten Boom on Forgiveness," *Guideposts Classics*, https://guideposts.org/positive-living/guideposts-classics-corrie-ten-boom-forgiveness/.

5. Fernando Lillo Redonet, "How Julius Caesar Started a Big War by Crossing a Small Stream," *National Geographic*, March/April 2017, https://www.nationalgeographic.com/history/history-magazine/article/julius-caesar-crossing-rubicon-rome.

ABOUT THE AUTHOR

O. S. Hawkins, a native of Fort Worth, Texas, is a graduate of Texas Christian University (BBA) and Southwestern Baptist Theological Seminary (MDiv, PhD). He is the former pastor of the historic First Baptist Church in Dallas, Texas, and is president emeritus of GuideStone Financial Resources, the world's largest Christian-screened mutual fund, serving 250,000 church workers and Christian university personnel with an asset base exceeding twenty billion dollars, where he served as president/CEO from 1997 to 2022. Hawkins is the author of more than fifty books, including the bestselling *The Joshua Code* and the entire Code Series of devotionals published by HarperCollins/Thomas Nelson, with sales of more than two million copies. He preaches in churches and conferences across the nation. He is married to his wife, Susie, and has two daughters, two sons-in-law, and six grandchildren. Visit him at OSHawkins.com and follow him on Twitter @OSHawkins.

TRANSFORM THE HEARTS OF YOUR CONGREGATION WITH

God's Word

The Joshua Code features 52 essential verses addressing challenges everyone deals with including: temptation, understanding salvation, prayer, grace, vision, integrity, and more. Perfect for a year-long preaching program, a personal devotional guide, or a gift to introduce friends and family to the Christian faith.

One hundred percent of the author's royalties and proceeds go to support Mission:Dignity—a ministry providing support for impoverished retired pastors and missionaries.

2 THE MOST OFTEN QUOTED VERSE IN THE BIBLE

"For God so loved the world that He gave His only begotten Son, that whoever believes in Him should not perish but have everlasting life."

JOHN 3:16

*I*f we ever memorize a verse of Scripture, it will most likely be John 3:16. It is the verse most often heard in the simplicity and beauty of a little child's voice proudly reciting it from memory. It is the one verse showing up on large placards at football games and other major sporting events. Those signs are located where television cameras cannot avoid its message. This is the one verse that has been spoken by many older saints as they breathed their final breath. It is the entire gospel in a nutshell.

Angel Martinez, the late evangelist who had memorized the entire New Testament, referred to John 3:16 as salvation's formula and observed that it contained four very insightful truths. It is the gospel in one verse. It reveals to us salvation's cause, its cost, its condition, and its consequence.

SALVATION'S CAUSE
"For God so loved the world"

The motivating factor behind God's redemptive plan for every man and woman is His love for us. He not only loves us, He *so* loves us! Later, the apostle Paul sought to describe this love by speaking of its "breadth, and length, and depth, and height" (Ephesians 3:18 KJV), "God is love" (1 John 4:16), and this deep emotion is what brings about the possibility of our redemption; knowing Him in the intimate relationship of Father and child. God's love for you is the motivating cause of salvation. "For God *so* loved . . ."

SALVATION'S COST
"that He gave His only begotten Son"

Our salvation, the free pardoning of our sin, and the promise of abundant and eternal life in Christ did not come without cost. Freedom is never free; it is always bought with blood. From the early chapters of Genesis, there is a scarlet thread woven throughout the pages of Scripture revealing the blood atonement. It climaxes in the final and complete sacrifice for sin on a Roman cross outside the city gates of Jerusalem. Jesus not only spoke of His love for us, "but God demonstrates His own love toward us, in that while we were still sinners, Christ died for us" (Romans 5:8). Our salvation in Christ came at a great cost: God "gave His only begotten Son."

SALVATION'S CONDITION
"that whoever believes in Him"

Salvation is not spelled "d-o," but "d-o-n-e." Many people, however, think their own good works are the pathway to eternal life. Consequently, they do this or do that, or they don't do this or don't do that, all in order to earn salvation. But our salvation is done. It is already purchased for us with the blood of Christ on the cross. Our part is to believe, to transfer our trust from ourselves and our own efforts to His finished work on the cross of Calvary.

To believe does not mean to simply give intellectual assent to the claims of Christ. It means to transfer our trust to Him alone for our salvation. The most pointed question in the entire Bible is asked of the apostle Paul by a Philippian jailer: "What must I do to be saved?" (Acts 16:30). Paul's immediate reply follows in the next verse: "Believe on the Lord Jesus Christ, and you will be saved." I believe *in* George Washington, but I don't believe *on* him; I don't trust my life to him. Salvation's condition is through faith—and faith alone—in the finished work of the Lord Jesus Christ.

SALVATION'S CONSEQUENCE
"should not perish but have everlasting life"

What a consequence! What a promise! Those without Christ are perishing, but those in Christ have the eternal promise of "everlasting life." This comes not from our own

human efforts, morals, or good deeds, but the promise is to those who realize that God's love reaches down to us, was made possible through the payment of Christ, and is received by grace through faith alone; believing in the Lord Jesus Christ.

An unknown, yet wise old sage once explained John 3:16 like this:

> *For God* . . . the greatest Lover
> *so loved* . . . the greatest degree
> *the world* . . . the greatest company
> *that He gave* . . . the greatest act
> *His only begotten Son* . . . the greatest gift
> *that whoever* . . . the greatest opportunity
> *believes* . . . the greatest simplicity
> *in Him* . . . the greatest attraction
> *should not perish* . . . the greatest promise
> *but* . . . the greatest difference
> *have* . . . the greatest certainty
> *everlasting life* . . . the greatest possession

As you memorize this old and oft-repeated verse this week, meditate on the fact that love is always something you do and remember that "God so loved the world that He gave." Yes, God knows you, loves you, and has a wonderful plan for your life.

YOU CAN
Count on God

Do you trust in the promises of God you've read in the Bible? Do you live your life by them? Join O. S. Hawkins in *The Promise Code* as he dives into 40 of those promises, giving them context and meaning.

ISBN: 978-1-4002-3524-7

One hundred percent of the author's royalties and proceeds go to support Mission:Dignity—a ministry providing support for impoverished retired pastors and missionaries.

THOMAS NELSON
Since 1798

2 THE PROMISE OF HIS ALL-SUFFICIENT GRACE

"My grace is sufficient for you, for My strength is made perfect in weakness."

—2 CORINTHIANS 12:9

*N*one of us are immune to disappointments and defeats, heartaches and heartbreaks, struggles and setbacks. These trials will affect each of us at one time or another. In fact, behind some of the most radiant lives I have known have been some of the biggest challenges. The great apostle Paul attested to this fact in his second letter to the Corinthians. He had a problem, and he had asked the Lord on three different occasions to remove it. Yet it was still there. This same man who had written to the Romans saying, "We are more than conquerors through Him who has loved us" (Romans 8:37), this same man who had said, "All things work together for good" (Romans 8:28), laid bare his heart in admission that he had a situation in which he could find no relief.

THE PROBLEM

His explanation began with *a problem*. He referred to his problem as "a thorn in the flesh" (2 Corinthians 12:7). What this "thorn" actually was no one knows for sure. But it was something physical in nature. It was a thorn in the "flesh." Some have speculated it was his physical appearance. After all, "his bodily presence [was] weak" (2 Corinthians 10:10). He had been lashed with a Roman whip almost two hundred times, he had been stoned at least three times—and once left for dead—and virtually every bone in his body had been fractured. Others contend his "thorn" was epilepsy. Still others speculate it was his failing eyesight, for earlier he had written to the Galatians saying, "See with what large letters I have written to you with my own hand!" (6:11). He had stated to them that he was confident that "if possible, you would have plucked out your own eyes and given them to me" (Galatians 4:15). Whatever it was, it was so irritating to him that he saw it as a problem and as an impediment to his work.

THE PURPOSE

But behind it all was *a purpose*. He had asked the Lord not once, not twice, but three times to remove it from him. But God did not remove it, for He had a greater purpose in it. Consider Paul's words: "Lest I should be exalted above measure by the abundance of the revelations, a thorn in the flesh was given to me" (2 Corinthians 12:7). Paul knew that this problem was "given" to him by God. God had big plans for

> Paul knew that this problem was "given" to him by God.

Paul. He later went from this experience to take the gospel to the entire Mediterranean world and ended up giving us half our New Testament through his own pen.

Haven't most of us been there, having something, or someone, who becomes a "thorn" in our own flesh? Perhaps, like Paul, we have asked the Lord repeatedly to free us from the problem only to find that it had been "given to us" by the Lord Himself to keep us humble and to fulfill His own purpose in our lives. Paul realized there was a divine purpose in his debilitating problem, and primarily it was to keep him from a sense of self-importance and self-exaltation.

THE PROMISE

Even though God did not answer Paul as he had hoped, He did something better. He gave him *a promise*: "He said to me, 'My grace is sufficient for you, for My strength is made perfect in weakness'" (2 Corinthians 12:9). God's grace is always enough—more than enough—for whatever need we may face. After all, grace is best defined as getting what we do not deserve. This is what distinguishes grace from mercy. Mercy is not getting what we do deserve. God is rich in grace and showers us daily with blessings we do not deserve. Earlier in the Corinthian letter Paul had said, "For you know the grace of our Lord Jesus Christ, that though He was rich, yet for your sakes He became poor, that you through His poverty might become rich" (2 Corinthians 8:9).

Perhaps even as you read these words, your own heart is heavy, and you have your own "thorn in the flesh" distracting you. In his epistle in the New Testament, James reminded us that "He [God] gives more grace . . . God resists the proud, but gives grace to the humble" (James 4:6). Whoever you are, whatever your circumstance, wherever you may reside, and with whomever you may have conflict, you can rest and rely on the promise that God's grace is sufficient.

THE POSSIBILITY

Finally, Paul left us with *a possibility* of much-needed strength that can actually come from weakness. We do not have to be strong. We can be weak, and in our own weakness we can find supernatural strength to meet the challenges of the day. Paul moved from being obsessed with his problem, asking the Lord repeatedly to take it away to no avail, to saying, "Therefore most gladly I will rather boast in my infirmities, that the power of Christ may rest upon me. . . . For when I am weak, then I am strong" (2 Corinthians 12:9–10).

There is a strange kinship between

> We can be weak, and in our own weakness we can find supernatural strength to meet the challenges of the day.

Paul's thorns and the thorns that pierced the brow of our Lord. Jesus, in weakness, with thorns in His brow and spikes nailed through His hands and feet, became strong. Could it be that every time Paul sensed the pressure of his thorn it reminded him of the power of the cross? There is nothing lovely about a crown of thorns. There may be nothing lovely about the thorn that irritates you. The cross was a cruel and harsh thing. Your thorn may be all of that to you. But before we turn the page to the next chapter, there is a final word to add. Paul said of his thorn that it "was given to me" (2 Corinthians 12:7). Make sure you are not trying to rid yourself of the very thing God "has given" you for His own purpose in your life. Then, stand on His promise: "My grace is sufficient for you."

—— A PROMISE AND A PRAYER ——

God is able to make all grace abound toward you,
that you, always having all sufficiency in all things,
may have an abundance for every good work.
2 CORINTHIANS 9:8

Lord, Your love has no limit, Your grace has no measure. You are all I need, always and in all ways. Your grace is sufficient for me. In Jesus' name, amen.